No-Till Gardening for Beginners

The Complete Guide to No-Till Growing
for an Organic, Bountiful, and Healthy Vegetable Garden
with No Tilling and Minimal Weeding

Max Barnes

© COPYRIGHT 2023 MAX BARNES - ALL RIGHTS RESERVED.

The content contained within this book may not be reproduced, duplicated or transmitted without direct written permission from the author or the publisher.

Under no circumstances will any blame or legal responsibility be held against the publisher, or author, for any damages, reparation, or monetary loss due to the information contained within this book. Either directly or indirectly.

Legal Notice:

This book is copyright protected. This book is only for personal use. You cannot amend, distribute, sell, use, quote or paraphrase any part, or the content within this book, without the consent of the author or publisher.

Disclaimer Notice:

Please note the information contained within this document is for educational and entertainment purposes only. All effort has been executed to present accurate, up to date, and reliable, complete information. No warranties of any kind are declared or implied. Readers acknowledge that the author is not engaging in the rendering of legal, financial, medical or professional advice. The content within this book has been derived from various sources. Please consult a licensed professional before attempting any techniques outlined in this book.

By reading this document, the reader agrees that under no circumstances is the author responsible for any losses, direct or indirect, which are incurred as a result of the use of the information contained within this document, including, but not limited to, — errors, omissions, or inaccuracies.

Your Free Gift

I'd like to offer you a gift as a way of saying thank you for purchasing this book. It's the eBook called 5 Easy Ways to Preserve Your Harvest. Sooner or later, you'll reach a point where you're able to grow more vegetables and fruits than you can eat, so I've created this book to help you preserve your harvest so that you could enjoy it later. You can get your free eBook by scanning the QR code below with your phone camera and joining our community. Alternatively, please send me an email to **maxbarnesbooks@gmail.com** and I will send you the free eBook.

SPECIAL BONUS!
Want this book for free?

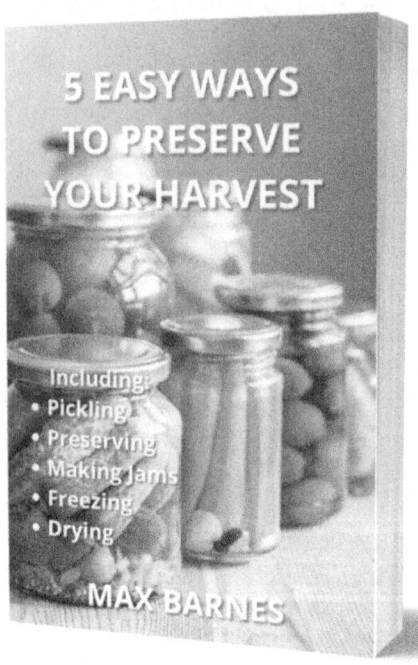

Get FREE unlimited access to it and all of my new books by joining our community!

Scan with your phone camera to join!

Garden Planner, Journal and Log Book

Keeping a journal to keep track of your garden and plants can help you determine what worked well and what didn't so that you can repeat your successes and avoid mistakes in the future. To help you plan your garden as well as keep all the important information about your garden and plants in one convenient place in an organized manner, I've created a garden planner, journal, and log book. Please scan the QR code below to find out more. Alternatively, please send me an email to **maxbarnesbooks@gmail.com** and I will send you the link to the journal.

Scan with your phone camera to find out more

Contents

Introduction 7
  What This Book Will Cover 7
  Why I'm Writing This Book 8

Chapter 1: No-Till Gardening Basics 9
  What Is No-Till Gardening? 9
  Principles of No-Till Gardening 9
  Benefits of No-Till Gardening 11

Chapter 2: Planning Your Garden 14
  Choosing the Perfect Location for Your Garden
  14
  Evaluating Sun Requirements and Exposure 17
  Determining When to Plant Your Garden 18
  Gardening Tools 21

Chapter 3: Starting Your Garden 26
  Starting from Scratch 26
  Transitioning to No-Till 28
  Starting a Raised Bed Garden 31
  Checking and Changing Soil pH Level 35

Chapter 4: Seeding and Transplanting 37
  Selecting and Starting Seeds 37
  Growing and Transplanting Seedlings 41
  Propagating Plants from Cuttings 44

Chapter 5: Maintaining Your Garden .. 48
  Watering 48
  Mulching 51
  Weeding 52
  General Garden Maintenance and Care 53

Chapter 6: Soil Fertility Management .. 59
  What Is Soil Fertility? 59
  Fertilizing 60
  Compost 62
  Intercropping and Companion Planting 64
  Cover Cropping 66
  Crop Rotation 67

Chapter 7: Pest Control and Dealing with Diseases 71
  Common Garden Pests 71
  Organic Pest Control Methods 78
  Using Trap Crops to Control Pests 82
  Dealing With Diseases 84
  Disease Prevention 92
  Companion Planting for Disease Management .. 93

Chapter 8: Time to Harvest the Bounty
  95
  When and How to Harvest Your Vegetables 95
  Storing Your Harvest 99

Chapter 9: Plant Profiles 104
  Vegetables 104
  Fruits 115
  Herbs 119
  Flowers 123

Conclusion 126

Resources 127

Index 132

Introduction

You may be wondering what is so wonderful about no-till gardening? It helps improve your soil structure by minimizing soil disturbance, which means you get better, more fertile soil and more abundant harvests for years to come with less work and without having to use heavy machinery. No-till gardening will help you improve your soil structure, texture, and drainage, keep the soil nice and moist, and also prevent soil erosion. It will help eliminate or greatly reduce the need for weeding. You will get more abundant harvests year after year, and all of that with less work and without the use of heavy machinery. It seems incredible to believe that you can reap all these benefits while actually doing less hard work. But it's true, and this book will help you learn how to do it with ease and effectively.

Many people want to grow their own food in the garden, but they're often unsure about where to start. Beginners can feel overwhelmed when they think about vegetable gardening and assume it's too complicated because they either don't have the knowledge about gardening or they mistrust the information they find online because it has conflicting information and doesn't look like it's from a reputable, quality source. This book will teach beginners to gardening everything they need to know about starting their own garden and growing vegetables organically and efficiently using no-till gardening techniques.

What This Book Will Cover

Chapter 1 will help you understand what no-till gardening is, its main principles, and the benefits of it.

Chapter 2 will help you plan your garden, including everything from choosing the perfect location to evaluating sun exposure and making decisions about when to plant your garden.

Chapter 3 is all about starting your garden either from scratch or transitioning to no-till if you have an existing garden, plus it will cover building raised beds if you'd prefer to go that route.

Chapter 4 will look at starting seeds and transplanting seedlings. It will also cover propagating plants from cuttings.

Chapter 5 will cover everything you need to know about maintaining your garden, looking at watering, mulching, weeding, and general garden maintenance and care.

Chapter 6 will give you information on soil fertility management, covering techniques such as fertilizing, making and using compost, intercropping and companion planting, cover cropping, and crop rotation, all of which will help improve and maintain your soil fertility in the long term.

Chapter 7 will cover pest control and dealing with diseases using organic options as well as disease prevention.

Chapter 8 will let you know the best time to harvest your vegetables, fruits, and herbs and provide information on how to store them.

Chapter 9 contains plant profiles that provide detailed information on how to grow various vegetables, fruits, herbs, and flowers. This is intended as a useful reference resource for you to refer back to when required.

Why I'm Writing This Book

My name is Max. I grew up on a farm as a child, and helping my grandmother Anna with her garden is one of my earliest childhood memories. My grandmother was very much ahead of her time and was very innovative. She experimented with different gardening methods, and I learned from this and continued to do this myself all throughout my adult life. I grow the majority of plants we eat on my property using different methods, including no-till. No-till gardening helps me live a sustainable lifestyle and get the best from my crops by keeping the soil healthy and fertile, which allows plants to thrive and provide abundant harvests year after year.

When I'm in my garden, it always brings back fond childhood memories of helping my grandmother on her farm. I learned so much about gardening in general, and no-till gardening in particular, from my grandmother. Throughout my adult life and up until this day, I have continued to keep my knowledge up-to-date, and I keep experimenting with different gardening methods so that I am able to grow a variety of plants all year round—lovely, delicious organic vegetables, fruits, and herbs that make our mealtimes a delight!

I am enthusiastic about gardening, and no-till gardening in particular, because it has so many incredible benefits. I want to show people that no-till gardening is not difficult, and that the benefits of doing it far outweigh the time, money, and effort invested. It will get you better, healthier crops, and it will help you live a healthier and more sustainable lifestyle, plus it's much better for the environment too.

I've learned a lot from my grandmother. I've kept a garden all my life, and it's been key to the sustainable lifestyle we live. I want to share my knowledge on how to live more sustainably with others who have an interest in it. Over the years, I've learned a lot: what not to do and pitfalls to avoid and things that are good to do that can help reap great benefits. I'd like to help people avoid the mistakes I've made and get there a little quicker using the useful tips, tricks, and techniques I've come across during all the years I've been keeping a garden. I've had a lot of help with no-till gardening from my grandmother as well as my friends and colleagues from whom I've learned over the years, and I'd like to give back and share some of that knowledge.

This book is a guide to organic vegetable gardening using no-till techniques. It is not a guide to anything else outside the realm of no-till growing and vegetable gardening.

Without further ado, let's jump into Chapter 1 and learn all about what no-till gardening is to get you started on your journey to what I personally think is the best way to grow vegetables.

Chapter 1: No-Till Gardening Basics

If you've ever tried to grow your own food, you're likely always on the lookout for techniques that can simplify gardening, which can sometimes be a grueling chore. While you may enjoy certain things about gardening, such as pruning your plants, watering and fertilizing them, and perhaps the most enjoyable thing—harvesting, digging is definitely the part that most people hate. Digging is done to loosen and aerate the soil, and it's often considered a necessity when it comes to preparing garden beds for new plants. But not only can it lead to back and joint pain and even blisters when performed at length, it's also not that good for your soil.

Don't get me wrong, digging does have certain benefits, such as loosening up and aerating soil and helping organic matter, like crop residue and weeds, decompose faster. However, disturbing the soil by digging can damage the soil structure and lead to soil compaction, which means plants' roots will have a harder time permeating the compacted soil. It can also harm the microorganisms living in it, which play an important role in maintaining a healthy soil environment. Digging can lead to increased weed growth, as you can expose weed seeds when digging and turning over soil. So, in many cases, digging can actually do more harm than good.

Fortunately, there is a method that eliminates the need for digging all together, and it's called no-till gardening (also known as no-dig gardening). It is more than just a way to skip over the mundane chore of digging your soil, though. This technique, which involves layering cardboard, compost, and organic matter, like straw, protects important microorganisms in your soil, reduces the number of weeds you get, and minimizes soil erosion. Though it requires some work and patience at first, in the long run, no-till gardening is easier, less time consuming, and more beneficial to your garden ecosystem.

What Is No-Till Gardening?

No-till gardening, also known as no-dig gardening, is essentially avoiding the intentional disruption of soil. Rather than using spades or plows to dig and turn over soil, it is more or less left alone. Instead of preparing the soil by digging or turning it over, no-till gardening builds up the soil through the application and decomposition of organic materials, such as compost, mulch, and cover crops. These layers break down to create a fantastic growing environment for your plants.

Principles of No-Till Gardening

Although no-till gardening involves different techniques and can manifest itself in many different shapes and forms, there are certain basic principles that prevail throughout. The main principles of no-till gardening are disturbing the soil as little as possible, keeping it covered and planted as much as possible, constantly adding organic matter, and choosing methods that are ecologically and financially sound on your scale, all of which will be covered below.

1. Disturbing the Soil as Little as Possible

No-till gardening is all about minimizing disturbance of the soil whenever possible, leaving the underground structure strong and intact. Soil is far more complex than just dirt, compost, and earthworms—

it's like a thriving underground "city" with billions of microorganisms, waterways, air spaces, nutrients, plants' roots, and networks. Every soil organism has a function, like breaking down decomposing organic matter or making nutrients available to plants.

Whenever we dig or till the soil and break it into pieces, we disturb or destroy the foundation of that underground "city," literally eliminating the "homes" where organisms live. So, one of the most important principles of no-till gardening is doing everything you can to maintain the natural underground structure and help the microorganisms in the soil thrive.

No-till methods help preserve the underground "city" structure so that microbes can keep the soil healthy. And in turn, this builds a resilient ecosystem that minimizes the need for fertilizers, pesticides, weed killers, and other interventions. Essentially, no-till methods allow the soil to function naturally without as much work from humans.

2. Keeping the Soil Covered as Much as Possible

In nature, soil is rarely left exposed. Bare soil is vulnerable to erosion by wind and storms and compaction from rain. In addition to that, sun is the ultimate sanitizer, so the soil must remain covered to preserve the natural underground ecosystem so that it can function at its highest level. In nature, soil is protected with a carpet of plant species that hold the dirt in place. This is why pioneer species, such as lichens, mosses, and commonly known weeds, like dandelions, quickly try to colonize bare soil.

If you think of soil as the skin of the Earth, you will realize that it needs a protective barrier to keep the underground ecosystem functioning properly. No-till gardening uses different techniques, such as mulching, cover cropping, and succession planting to maintain coverage. This helps protect the soil from erosion and compaction and also helps improve soil quality, as both organic mulch and finished cover crops will decompose and enrich the soil with nutrients.

3. Keeping the Soil Planted as Much as Possible

There is perhaps nothing more beneficial to soil microorganisms than living plant roots. The root zone, also called the rhizosphere, is the primary habitat for beneficial bacteria and fungi where they can thrive. You will recall from biology class that plants' leaves convert sunlight and carbon dioxide through photosynthesis into delicious treats on which beneficial fungi and bacteria feed and grow. However, without roots in the soil, these beneficial microorganisms die out. If you rip out the roots between every crop, you also take the rhizosphere ecosystems with them. The microbial populations left in the soil will then need some time to recover before repopulating new roots.

This is why keeping the soil planted as much as possible is one of the principles of no-till gardening. A continuous presence of living roots ensures that the microorganisms is the soil can thrive and easily "hop" from old crops to new ones. Growing year-round is not necessary, and it's not always practical, but it's certainly advantageous, so having something growing as much as possible is often a significant goal for no-till growers. There are different methods to achieve this, such as cover cropping, succession planting, and perennial ground cover, all of which help maintain the soil ecosystem as well as protect the soil from erosion and compaction.

4. Constantly Adding Organic Matter

The overarching theme through all of the above practices is adding organic matter. Organic matter is perhaps the most valuable part of your soil ecosystem. It includes all decomposed, carbon-rich materials of once-living plants or animals.

Tilling and digging damage and essentially burn up your organic matter, reducing soil quality over the years. This has happened in the Midwestern United States, where the rich topsoil was once over 20 feet (6 m) deep. Much of that topsoil is now less than 3 feet (0.9 m) deep and extremely degraded due to constant tillage and chemical use. No-till methods, however, improve your soil quality and add to the reservoir of organic matter instead of burning it up. By using no-till methods, you can lead a more sustainable lifestyle because the soil will produce good vegetables for you and your family for decades to come.

5. Making a Living

A lot of homesteaders and backyard gardeners may choose not to use tillage, and this is often as much a practical choice (because getting a tractor or a tiller into a yard is pricy and/or inconvenient) as an ecological one.

For production agriculture, however, farmers have to scale that idea to be efficient and profitable. After all, making a living is the main goal of a no-till farmer. So, the most important guiding principle in no-till market gardening is that one's methods must be profitable for the farmer and soil alike. You may have noticed that all the principles above are not absolute—you should disturb the soil as little as possible or keep it covered and planted as much as possible, which means you can choose how far you want to go with different principles. Of course, keeping the soil planted all year round is best, but it's neither the most practical nor the most economical choice in some cases. So, you can choose a method that is ecologically and financially sound on your scale and enjoy the fruits of your labor.

Benefits of No-Till Gardening

No-till gardening has a lot of great benefits, which will be covered below.

1. Improving Soil Structure, Aeration, and Drainage

Earthworms, bacteria, and other microorganisms are important to healthy soil structure—their tunnels provide aeration and drainage, and their excretions bind together soil crumbs. Digging soil disturbs them, and restoring the natural balance takes months. No-till gardening helps preserve the natural balance by minimizing soil disturbance, which in turn leads to improving natural soil aeration and drainage, and as a result, better soil quality and fertility.

2. Preventing Soil Compaction and Erosion

Digging and tilling the soil can lead to soil compaction, which means plants' roots will have a harder time permeating the soil, so you'll get poor harvests. No-till gardening helps prevent soil compaction, since the soil is mostly left alone, plus constantly adding organic matter, which is one of the main principles of no-till gardening, further helps improve soil structure, aeration, and drainage and helps microorganisms in the soil thrive.

Soil erosion is the removal of the top layer of the soil due to physical forces, such as strong winds, hard rains, and flowing water. Disturbing the soil by digging or tilling promotes soil erosion because it exposes the loose soil and makes it bare, making it an easy target for wind and water erosion. So, leaving the soil undisturbed using the no-till method helps prevent soil erosion. In addition, cover cropping is often used in no-till gardening, which helps prevent soil erosion by having cover crops in place when garden beds are not used to grow vegetable crops, for example, over the winter.

3. Reducing or Eliminating Need for Weeding

There are weed seeds in most garden soils that lay dormant until the soil is disturbed and the seeds become exposed to light. With no-till gardening, you don't need to dig or turn over the soil, so these seeds will remain dormant indefinitely. Of course, some weeds will still appear, as weed seeds can be transferred by wind or birds. However, one of the main principles of no-till gardening is keeping the soil covered with mulch, which helps noticeably reduce the number of weeds you get because weed seeds will land on the mulch and won't be able to get to the soil and germinate. Even if you get a few weeds here and there, it's easy to remove them by hand if you pull them early in the morning or shortly after watering while the soil is damp.

4. Increasing Soil Moisture and Saving Water

As mentioned previously, one of the main principles of no-till gardening is keeping your soil covered with mulch. Not only does it help prevent weeds from growing, but it also helps keep the moisture in the soil and reduce the amount of water lost due to evaporation.

5. Less Hard Work and Fewer Tools

While starting a no-till garden takes a bit of work and preparation, you still don't need to wrangle around heavy equipment or work up a sweat as you work the soil. And once you have everything set up, maintaining a no-till garden is relatively simple, so you can sit back and enjoy all the benefits while doing less work. The hardest part of no-till gardening is perhaps hauling the occasional wheelbarrow of compost or chopping down finished or cover crops. You will no longer need to spend your time toiling with a shovel or rototiller or hunched over for hours pulling weeds.

6. Higher Crop Yields

As you now know, no-till gardening does a lot to help improve soil quality and fertility, so it's not a surprise that this also helps get higher yields. A 29-year-long study in the Midwest found that the no-till method helps consistently improve yields in the long term compared to standard tillage methods. The scientists came to a conclusion that the yield increases come mainly from greater moisture retention and higher levels of organic matter (Kellogg Biological Station, 2020). Both of these factors help support accelerated crop growth and greater resilience against environmental stressors, like drought or extreme weather.

Although it's likely you won't notice significant increases right after the initial transition to no-till, the first couple of years will set a solid foundation for skyrocketing garden harvests in the seasons to come. As your soil structure improves and beneficial microorganisms thrive, you can expect your harvests to increase noticeably and with considerably less work than with traditional gardening methods.

I first heard about no-till gardening from my grandma when I was a child and I was helping her around the garden. I do specifically recall my grandma never asking me to help her dig or till the garden. Instead, she lined the soil with cardboard and newspapers in order to eliminate weeds and then topped this with compost to add organic matter to the soil. I remember her being so proud she didn't have to spend hours digging or tilling and got incredible harvests year after year. As an adult, I continued researching the topic of no-till gardening further and applying it in my own garden, and I rapidly started to see the many benefits of this for the soil and for better, more abundant, and tastier crops. I have been using no-till methods in my own garden ever since.

Key takeaways from this chapter:

1. No-till gardening, also known as no-dig gardening, is essentially avoiding the intentional disruption of soil. Rather than using spades or plows to dig and turn over soil, it is more or less left alone. Instead of preparing the soil by digging or turning it over, no-till gardening builds up the soil through the application and decomposition of organic materials, such as compost, mulch, and cover crops. These layers break down to create a fantastic growing environment for your plants.

2. The main principles of no-till gardening are disturbing the soil as little as possible, keeping it covered and planted as much as possible, constantly adding organic matter, and choosing methods that are ecologically and financially sound on your scale.

3. No-till gardening has a lot of great benefits, including improving soil structure, aeration, and drainage, preventing soil compaction and erosion, reducing or eliminating need for weeding, increasing soil moisture and saving water, having to do less hard work and needing fewer tools, and enjoying higher crop yields.

Chapter 2: Planning Your Garden

So, now you know what no-till gardening is all about and its many benefits. You're probably feeling all enthused and ready to start your own garden. The next steps are to plan your garden to ensure it is a success. You may have lots of questions about how much sun your garden should get, how to find the perfect location for your garden, and when you should start planting. This chapter will help you choose the perfect location for your garden, evaluate sun requirements and exposure, determine when to plant your garden, and this will be discussed for in-ground gardens as well as raised bed gardens.

Choosing the Perfect Location for Your Garden

It's really important to find the perfect location for your garden prior to planting. In order to choose an ideal location, you need to consider the following:

Sun Exposure

The more direct sunlight per day your plants get, the better. Most plants need at least 6 hours of sunlight per day. Evaluating sun requirements and exposure will be covered in the next section of this chapter in more detail.

Water

Consider how easy it is to get water to where you plan to have your garden. Ideally, you want your vegetable garden to be near a water source because you'll need to water your plants weekly. If the weather is hot, you'll need to water your plants more often, and if you have a long way to fetch water, this makes it a more difficult task.

It's sensible to give some thought to water conservation. Consider if you could set up some water butts. Also, give thought to how to water your garden if you're ever away from home. Will a friend or a family member do this for you? You could also consider reservoirs with drip irrigation.

If you don't have access to an outside tap or water butts, then a hose is a really good addition to make watering your garden easier. If your property has a well, you could hook a hose directly to the well for watering. If you're thinking about watering your garden with a watering can, this will soon feel like a chore. Watering cans are heavy, and you'll need far more of them than you expect. This isn't meant to sound negative, but it is something to be aware of when considering where you will get water for your garden.

When watering your plants, you should try to water them at the base and avoid getting water on the leaves in order to avoid fungal diseases, which is why I would suggest avoiding sprinklers. You can opt for a drip irrigation system, though. Drip irrigation is a method for watering your garden that uses a system of pipes and valves connected to a water source, and it drips water onto the soil slowly. There are different types of drip irrigation systems, and this will be covered in more detail in Chapter 5.

Soil Quality

Soil is the very foundation of your garden, and it's important to always seek to improve and enrich it. Vegetables tend to like well-drained soil, which means that soil allows water to drain at a moderate rate and without water pooling and puddling. You need to ensure that there are no contaminants getting into your garden too. For example, sometimes sidewalks have ice melting treatments put on, and you don't want that running off into your vegetable garden.

If you have a lawn on your property, this can give you an indication of the health of your soil. If your lawn is lush and healthy, you probably have good soil. If your lawn is poor, your soil quality may need some work.

Even if your soil quality isn't great, don't worry—it's possible to improve it by adding organic matter. However, if the soil quality is really poor in your area, you could consider starting a raised bed garden. Raised beds are typically filled with topsoil, compost, and things like coconut coir and peat moss. Building and filling raised beds will be covered in detail in the next chapter.

Level Ground or a Gentle Slope

The ideal location for your vegetable garden would be on level ground or ground that has a very gentle slope. Try to avoid areas that stay wet throughout the spring or ground that is at the bottom of a slope because water will run downhill when you water your garden or when it rains. If the ground is always wet, the plants will suffer, and seeds or seedlings can get washed away.

Lower parts of your garden are cooler than upper slopes. South-facing areas are warmer than north-facing ones. If the land is on a hill, the soil will be shallow, and if it's in a valley, the soil will be deeper because of erosion from above.

Ease of Access

If you can easily get to your garden, this will make it easier for you to water, maintain, and harvest it. It should be as convenient as possible for you. It's wonderful if you're able to see your garden from your kitchen and makes it perfect to just pop out to snip off some herbs to use in your evening meal cooking.

Fencing

Having a fence helps protect your plants from wildlife, such as deer, rabbits, and other animals.

Protection From the Elements

If possible, try to ensure that your crops aren't battered by windy weather. Crops need some shelter, and this is especially true for tall crops that could bend or snap in the wind, like corn and sunflowers.

Walls and fences can help. If they have some gaps in them, this can be even better because the wind will filter through them. Certain tall plants that grow upright and produce fruit, like tomatoes, peppers, peas, beans, and eggplants, all benefit from an area that is not too windy so that they don't snap by being blown about.

Analyze the Environment

There may be things in your garden that can cause different conditions, so carefully analyze structures, trees and shrubs, and hard surfaces when you're considering a location for your garden.

You could have parts of your or your neighbor's property that casts shade. I have a part of my garden that is in the shade until later in the day just because of where the fence is. You should look at trees and hedges too. Some structures, like hedges, fences, and trees, may help protect your crops from strong winds, but they may also create shade or could become snow drift areas in the winter. Areas under trees may be warmer, but they will also likely be drier because the tree canopy may catch some of the rain. If you have hard surfaces, like rooftops, you could get water runoff from these, so do think carefully about where this water is running off onto so that you don't drown your plants.

Vegetables planted in the shade aren't as productive as those in full sun and may be more susceptible to diseases and pest damage. If you live somewhere exceptionally hot, then plants may need some shade in the summer. You can use a shade cloth or plant taller plants nearby to create some shade.

You can also consider which side of your garden faces north and which side faces south with regards to planting too. You can plant smaller crops in the south and taller plants in the north. For example, you can plant cabbage in the south and sugar snap peas in the north. This way, sugar snap peas won't cast too much shade on your cabbage.

Consider Time and Effort

It's highly likely you will need to prepare your land before you can plant your garden. You'll need to remove rocks, grass, and weeds. You'll need to prepare your garden beds by adding organic matter and compost. You may need to put up a fence to keep out wildlife. If you decide to go for a raised bed garden, you'll obviously need to build raised beds. You will also need to weed your garden periodically so that your plants (and not the weeds) get the nutrients they should. Gardening is enjoyable, but it's probably best to start small and grow gradually rather than have a garden that's too big for you to take care of that becomes onerous and a chore.

Enough Space Between Plants

Plants need room to breathe and have air circulating because this will help prevent mold, fungi, and mildew from attacking your plants. Having good airflow will also help keep pests away. Plant spacing requirements for different plants will be covered in Chapter 9.

Take Time to Check It's Safe to Dig

Check the plans of your house to see where pipes lay, or ask the local authorities. What you don't want to do is dig up a water or a gas pipe, or even worse, hit an underground electric line, which could be fatal.

Best Place for a Raised Bed Garden

You should consider the same factors when choosing a location for your raised beds as with an in-ground garden: you should consider the sunlight the area gets, wind exposure, how close it is to your home for convenience, whether there are any trees in close proximity, and how easy it will be to water it. You can also consider the aesthetics and how nice it looks, as it is meant to bring you pleasure and not be an eyesore.[1]

---

[1] Image from https://www.gardenary.com/blog/where-to-put-your-raised-beds-how-to-choose-the-ideal-location

Evaluating Sun Requirements and Exposure

All plants require a certain number of hours of daily exposure to sunlight in order to grow and thrive. When you purchase seeds, seedlings, or plants from a nursery, their ideal sunlight requirements are almost always printed on the seed packet, tag, or label. Most vegetables require at least 6 hours of sunlight per day to grow.

If you look at a seed packet or a plant label, you'll find the following terms that describe sun requirements:

- Full sun
- Full sun to partial shade
- Partial shade (or part shade)
- Dappled sun/shade
- Full shade

Full sun means that an area must receive 6–8 hours of direct sunlight on most days mostly between the hours of 10 a.m. and 4 p.m. Many plants need full sun to grow, flower, and produce fruit, but some plants can't handle the intense heat and/or dry conditions that often come with that much exposure to the sun. Mulching is one of the key principles of no-till gardening, and not only does it help prevent weeds from growing, but it also helps keep the soil cool and keep in moisture (this will be discussed in more detail later in the book). When you choose plants, do some research on the species to determine if there are limitations on their full sun requirement. Plants that are sensitive to heat will usually come with a caution that they require some shelter from direct sunlight in mid-afternoon in hot climates. One way around this is to place these sensitive plants where they receive most of their sunlight in the morning or very late afternoon when temperatures might be cooler. As long as the plants receive at least 6–8 hours of direct sunlight, they should grow well.

The terms "partial (or part) sun" and "partial (or part) shade" are essentially the same and are often used interchangeably. Partial sun or partial shade means that an area must get 4–6 hours of sun exposure per day, preferably in the cooler hours of the morning. There is a subtle difference between these two terms, though. Partial sun puts greater emphasis on plants receiving at least the minimum sun requirements of 4–6 hours. These plants are typically more resistant to heat and need sunlight to flower and produce fruit, just not as much as plants that need full sun. If they're not flowering or growing up to expectations, you can try moving them to a location that gets more sun. Partial shade means that plants don't tolerate heat as well as plants that need partial sun, and they may need some relief from heat, especially in the afternoon. You can place these plants where there is some shade, for example, near a tree or a fence or on the east side of a structure, which would typically be shaded in the afternoon.

Dappled sun is a rare term, but you might find it used to describe sun requirements of a few plants. Dappled sun is similar to partial shade, but it means the sunlight filters through the branches and foliage of deciduous trees. Deciduous trees shed their leaves annually. Woodland plants, such as trillium, Solomon's seal, and understory trees and shrubs, prefer dappled sun.

Full shade means that plants need 4 hours of sunlight mostly in the morning or late afternoon or a full day of dappled sunlight. Some people think that full shade means no sunlight at all, but that's not true. Very few plants, other than mushrooms, can survive without sunlight.

Direct sunlight means that sunlight is physically hitting the leaves of plants. Indirect sunlight can mean that sunlight is going through a window or through dappled leaves or is bouncing off walls to reach the plant. If somewhere is classed as shaded, it means that sunlight mostly doesn't reach the plants in this area.

Once you have considered the space you have, you then need to spend some time monitoring which areas of the space receive sun and make notes of how this changes throughout the course of a day. The best way to measure average sunlight exposure is to simply observe the area where you plan to start your garden every hour during the daylight hours over a week or two. Make notes to determine the average amount of sunlight the area receives each hour and where the shadows fall. Make notes whether it's full sun, filtered or dappled light, or full shade.

The path of the sun changes throughout the year, so it's best to measure the light in your garden during the growing season for your plants. You can make a note of how this changes over the seasons so that you're able to select the best plants for your garden.

You can also use flags or stakes to show the light and shadow in your yard. Or you could use some sheets of tracing paper and sketch the yard outline onto each page, then mark where the light and shade is every hour each time using a different sheet of tracing paper, and then you can layer the pages together to get an indication of how much light your yard receives.

If you don't personally have the time to monitor your garden each hour of the day, other options include purchasing a garden light meter, which may also measure soil moisture and pH levels too. Or you could take a picture of your garden every hour or set up a time-lapse camera that will do it for you. When you have a sun map, it's much easier to choose suitable plants for your garden by reading seed packets and seeing whether they like full sun, partial sun or shade, or full shade.

When you have determined the average amount of sunlight an area receives, you can choose plants that match the conditions your space has. If you don't have an environment that gets 6–8 hours of sunlight per day, then growing some vegetables may be tough, but you could still grow leafy greens, such as kale, spinach, Swiss chard, mustard greens, and lettuce, and also herbs, such as basil, parsley, mint, rosemary, oregano, thyme, sage, and chives. These leafy greens will give you so many good nutrients and vitamins, and herbs will really give your food a kick of flavor.

Determining When to Plant Your Garden

In the springtime, it can be tricky to determine when you should sow seeds or transplant seedlings outside because the weather can vary so much from being very cold and rainy one day to being warm and sunny the next day, and you can also still get some frost in the spring too. When you start to see signs of life in the spring, it can be easy to get too carried away and think you can plant right away, but there can still be some frosts, so you may be better off waiting a little.

Here are some tried and tested ways to know when to plant your garden:

Check The Seed/Plant Packaging

You will notice that on most seed packets it is suggested they should be sown after the last frost in your area. The last frost date refers to the average final spring frost in your area. Last frost dates are only an estimate based on historical climate data and are not set in stone. In the US, the National Weather Service tracks this data and has created charts that show the average last frost dates for various areas. You can find them by simply going online and typing in the phrase "last frost date by zip", and you'll find websites where you can check the last frost date for your specific zip code.

Check the Temperature of the Soil

Another way to determine when to plant your garden is by taking the temperature of the soil. Most seeds germinate when the soil temperature is between 60 and 85°F (15–30°C). If the soil temperature is below 50°F (10°C), most seeds won't germinate. You may find that raised beds warm up earlier than the soil in your garden does.

Succession Planting

Succession planting is the practice of seeding crops at intervals of 7 to 21 days in order to maintain a consistent supply of produce throughout the season. It also involves planting a new crop after harvesting the first crop.

Succession planting can be done in several different ways. You can plant the same vegetables with staggered plantings. This means spacing out plantings of the same vegetable every 2–4 weeks. Many vegetables fade after producing their initial crop, so rather than planting your entire row of beans all at once, you can plant part of the row at the beginning of the season and then plant more in about 2–4 weeks. This way, a new crop will be continually coming in. As the first plants start to flag, you can replant that area with beans or use it for a different crop.

You can plant different vegetables in succession. Some crops, such as peas, have a short growing season, and the space they were using can be replanted with later season crops, like eggplants.

You can grow the same vegetables with different maturity rates. Some vegetables have different varieties with different maturity rates, including early-, mid-, and late-season varieties. Sometimes this will be mentioned on the seed packet, and sometimes you will just have to read the "days to maturity" number. Vegetables with different maturity rates include pole beans, broccoli, Brussels sprouts, cabbage, carrots, cauliflower, celeriac, celery, collard greens, corn, eggplants, kale, melons, peas, summer squash, and tomatoes.

You can also pair vegetables in the same spot. This is known as intercropping, and it's an excellent way to squeeze even more productivity from your vegetable garden and maximize your growing space. It will be covered in detail in Chapter 6.

If you live in the US, there is the USDA Plant Hardiness Zone Map, which divides the US into 13 different zones that show the best time to start planting plants. You can find it online by searching "USDA Plant Hardiness Zone Map", or you could ask a county cooperative extension in your area for a local calendar to ensure you get planting timings right.

Hardy Crops

You would tend to plant mid-season crops in early spring, while in the summer you'd plant crops that you want to harvest in the fall. It is good advice to wait until there's no risk of frost. Once the soil is no longer frozen and can be worked (typically 4 weeks before the last frost), then you can start planting your plants.

Crops that can survive cold weather are planted first—they are known as hardy. Gardeners typically use the term "hardy" to describe a plant that can survive a freeze, frost, or a cold snap. Hardy crops include asparagus, broccoli, cabbage, garlic, kale, onions, peas, radishes, rhubarb, spinach, Swiss chard, and turnips. Some of these hardy crops (peas, cabbage, broccoli, radishes, and cauliflower) can also be planted in late summer for fall harvest.

While you can plant hardy crops early, there's no point in doing so if your soil is soaking wet. And while they'll put up with a bit of cold weather, they still won't germinate until the temperature is around 55°F (13°C). If you want an early harvest, you can start seedlings indoors early and then transplant them outside. You can buy frost covers at garden centers or online to protect your plants from an unexpected frost. Or if you don't have access to these, you could use a blanket or a piece of sack.

Half-Hardy Crops

Half-hardy crops can be planted after hardy crops. "Half-hardy" is a term used to describe plants that can survive only limited or light frost—meaning just an hour or two of frost or near-freezing temperatures. Half-hardy plants must be protected from anything more than a touch of frost. Half-hardy crops include artichokes, beets, carrots, cauliflower, celery, chard, chicory, Chinese cabbage, endive, lettuce, and potatoes.

Tender Crops

Tender crops do not do well in cold weather. "Tender" is a term used to describe plants that are injured by frost or cold weather. Tender plants must be protected from temperatures near freezing. So, you should ideally wait about 3–4 weeks after the last frost to plant these because some of them need the temperature to be at least 65°F (18°C) to grow, as they are susceptible to cold.

These include beans, corn, cucumbers, melons, okra, peppers, pumpkins, squash, sweet potatoes, and tomatoes. You can start most plants indoors and transplant them outside when the weather gets better. So, you could start growing seeds indoors 8–12 weeks before your expected last frost date. This will be covered in more detail in Chapter 4 of this book.

If it's currently early spring and you want a late spring harvest, then you could choose cool-season vegetables, such as kale, lettuce, spinach, peas, radishes, and broccoli. You could plant onions and potatoes to be harvested late summer to fall. If it's mid-spring and you want a summer harvest, then you could plant tomatoes, peppers, squash, cucumbers, eggplants, and melons. You can also get perennial plants (plants that live a few years), such as strawberries and asparagus, and these can give year upon year of fantastic produce.

Be Organized Throughout the Year

Generally, there is always something you can be doing throughout the year to prepare and be organized for gardening. You can plan where you'll place your vegetables in January (remembering to rotate crops from the previous year—this will be covered in more detail in Chapter 6). You can also make a list of what seeds you want to buy.

In February, you can order your seeds, and when they arrive, look at when they need to be sowed in the garden or started indoors, and work backwards to plan for this and organize them accordingly. Ensure you have seed starting trays, seed starting mix, and all the gardening tools you require. You could start planting asparagus, artichoke, horseradish, and rhubarb if the soil is warm enough. You can also start growing seeds for broccoli, lettuce, spinach, onions, cabbage, and kale inside at that time.

In March, you can start seeds indoors for tomatoes, peppers, squash, sweet corn, eggplants, snap beans, and pumpkins. If the soil temperature is above 40°F (5°C), you could start planting kale, lettuce, spinach, and onions. At the end of the month, you might be able to plant peas, provided that the soil is not too wet.

In April, it can still be cool, so you may need frost covers just in case of cold weather. You can keep checking the soil temperature, and when it gets above 60°F (18°C), you can transplant seedlings of radishes, onions, leeks, cabbage, beets, spinach, carrots, peas, and Brussels sprouts outside.

In May, you can plant everything else for the most part (or very early June if you're worried it may still be cold, depending on where you live). Soil temperature should be above 70°F (21°C) to plant tomatoes and peppers. You can also plant melons, eggplants, sweet corn, cucumbers, potatoes, and herbs. Always follow the instructions given on seed packets. Throughout June, you should be thinning some of your seedlings. You may need to stake up plants that require support.

In July, you could plant some more beans, carrots, cucumbers, and cauliflower where there is room to give you a late harvest. If you haven't planted for a fall harvest, it's not too late to do so in August. It's also worth making a note in a garden journal of what has worked well and what hasn't so that you can remember this next year when you come to plant your garden up. I have created a garden journal that will help you keep all the important information about your garden and plants in one convenient place. If you'd like to find out more about it, please check page 5 of this book, right before the table of contents.

In September, you may need to use frost sheets and covers to protect plants like tomatoes and keep them ripening on the vine. You could prepare new garden beds or build raised beds to be ready for springtime. If you have healthy looking herbs, you could put them in planters and put them inside over winter.

In October, you can continue to plant cool-season crops, such as cabbage, kale, cauliflower, beets, Brussels sprouts, broccoli, parsnips, celery, onions, peas, spinach, turnips, chives, parsley, radishes, lettuce, and Swiss chard.

Gardening Tools

There are so many tools you can buy in your local garden center that it's hard to figure out what you actually need in the garden. In this section, I'd like to cover the essential tools you will need as a gardener. I will also suggest a few tools that might be handy to have.

To explain why you need certain tools, we'll look at the whole process, from starting your garden to harvesting the delicious produce. This book is based on the no-dig method, so we'll follow the process of building your garden according to this method. It will be covered in-depth in Chapter 3, but in short, it involves covering the ground with cardboard to kill the weeds first, then layering compost, straw, and other organic materials, and finally, creating indentations for planting vegetables.

1. Gloves

Gardening is a lovely hobby, but it can quickly turn into a hassle without the right pair of gloves. Make sure to get gloves that are durable but not too bulky, especially for working with seeds or transplanting seedlings. Ensure they fit well too, as poorly fitting gloves can cause blisters or result in accidents from slipping off. The fabric should ideally be water resistant but also breathable—this will help keep your hands cool and comfortable. Longer cuffs will help protect your wrists and forearms from scratches and keep the soil from getting in.

2. Pitchfork

You'll need to move a lot of compost to build no-till garden beds, and a pitchfork is perfect for that. It's also great for turning your compost pile and moving loose materials.

3. Rake

Rake is used to create a level working area once you've layered your garden beds. A good rake should have a sturdy handle, and the prongs should be made out of one piece of metal. Raking is all about spreading out topsoil to create a level surface and also loosening the topsoil to prepare garden beds for planting. This helps improve drainage and prevent water logging issues, and it also allows for better water absorption in the soil.

4. Trowel

So, your bed is leveled and ready for some transplants. For this, you can use a trowel. I'd suggest getting a high-quality trowel because cheaper ones may look good at first glance, but they break or bend easily and will probably not last you one season. This will be your tool for moving small amounts of soil, transplanting your vegetables, and weeding in tight spaces where it's hard to use a hoe.

5. Hoe

Garden hoes come in many different varieties: Dutch hoe, draw hoe, heart-shaped hoe, and more. The most common is the Dutch hoe. But we mainly use a straight hoe. Stirrup or shuffle hoes are great for shallow hoeing—it's a technique for weeding, and this will be covered in more detail in Chapter 5.

A hoe is a great tool for getting rid of weeds. To use your hoe for weeding, hold it as you would hold a broom, and angle it so the blade goes just below the surface. This way, you can slice off the tops from weeds.

6. Watering Can

As mentioned previously, there are a lot of ways to water your garden, and watering it using watering cans can be a daunting task. However, it can be fine if you have a smaller garden, and especially if you have a water butt so that you don't have to carry heavy watering cans from your house. Even though watering by hand can be quite a task, it's also a good moment to inspect your vegetables and your soil, picking out some weeds as you go.

7. Pruners/Scissors

Pruners come in really handy when it's time to harvest your crop. You don't need to get really expensive ones. Just make sure they have a comfortable grip and look like they won't fall apart after one use.

There are two main styles of pruners: bypass and anvil. In bypass pruners, blades bypass each other to make the cut. In anvil pruners, blade slams on top of a ridge. I personally prefer bypass pruners because they seem to cut cleaner, and it's important to make clean cuts with your pruners so that you don't hurt your plants. Pruners need to be kept sharp, so if a blade goes dull, sharpen or replace it because dull pruners can damage plants.

8. Spade/Shovel

Even though no-till gardening is about trying to disturb the soil as little as possible, you might have to do some digging when dealing with bigger plants or trees that you'd like to plant in the garden. For this, you can either get a spade or a shovel. I personally prefer a spade because it's made to really get in the soil and dig it up. Some spades have bend-over tops to rest your foot on, which makes them a bit more comfortable to use. With no-till gardening, you won't have to use it much, so your spade will probably last you a lifetime.

9. Broadfork

This is also sometimes called a U-fork or grelinette, and this is a garden tool used to manually break up compacted soil to improve aeration and drainage. Broadforks are often used as part of no-till garden bed preparation process because they preserve the soil structure and avoid the resurfacing of weed seeds. It typically consists of five or so metal tines spaced a few inches apart on a horizontal bar with two handles extending upwards to chest or shoulder level that form a large U-shape. Using a broadfork is rather simple—you just need to drop it in, step on the horizontal bar, and lightly pull backward on the handles to lift the tines upward. Then, you simply move the broad fork back about a foot (30 cm) and repeat the process. If you have compacted soil, you should get a 14-16-inch-deep (35–40 cm) broadfork. If you have relatively loose soil or raised beds, then 10–12-inch-long (25–30 cm) tines are just fine.

In the first couple of years after transitioning to no-till, you may need to use the broadfork several times to break up soil compaction. With time, as the soil becomes looser and healthier, you won't have to use it anymore.

10. Dibber

Dibbers are used to make holes when planting seeds or transplanting seedlings. You can use a trowel for transplanting seedlings, but a dibber can come in really handy. You simply need to put some weight on it, and you'll make a nice gap for your transplants—it's really easy to pop in your plants this way.

11. Hedge Shears

Hedge shears are meant to trim hedges, but they are a great tool for trimming or cutting down plants around the garden. After the harvest, for most plants it's time to go, so you can pull them out or cut them down with shears and add them to your compost pile. I usually cut the plants down because roots will decompose and feed the soil, so hedge shears come in really handy.

12. Wheelbarrow

If you have a bigger garden, you'll need to move quite a lot of compost and mulch around, so a wheelbarrow will definitely come in handy. You'll need it only sporadically, though, so that's something to think about. Think if you could borrow one for a few days—this will help you save some money and space. If you decide to get a wheelbarrow, make sure it stays inside when not using it. That's all you need to do to keep it for many years. If your shed is small, you can also "park" it with the handles turned up against the wall.

When I was planning our garden, initially we didn't have an outdoor tap, which meant that every time I wanted to water the plants, I had to carry watering cans from my kitchen through my front room and out the patio doors to the garden.

We then had a couple of water butts set up in the garden that collect rainwater, and this made watering the garden so much easier. I could fill two watering cans simultaneously with lovely natural rainwater. There are no chemicals added to it, which may not be the case with tap water sometimes, so it's better for plants and soil. It's also better financially because rainwater is essentially free.

The location I chose to start our garden in gets a good 8–10 hours of direct sunlight a day. I had taken the time to evaluate sun exposure using a sun map prior to planting my garden, and I do this at the start of each new season just to ensure that all my plants are planted in the best place and get enough sunlight or shade, whichever they require. The garden is right outside the patio doors of our house, so it's very easy to get to. It is also fenced, so wildlife can't easily get in, though we do get an occasional hedgehog or a toad, which is great because they eat slugs and insects.

Key takeaways from this chapter:

1. Location: When choosing the perfect location for your garden, you need to ensure the spot you pick gets at least 6–8 hours of direct sunlight. It needs to be a space that is easy to get water to. If your soil isn't great, you can improve it by adding organic matter. The garden space needs to be convenient for you to get to, and ideally, it needs to be fenced off. Your garden needs protection from the elements so that your plants are not battered by the wind. The ground should be level or with a gentle slope. Look at the environment around your garden to see where shade is cast. Give thought to the time and effort that gardening takes and start off with a sensibly sized garden that will not become a chore—this should be something that you get enjoyment from. Next, ensure that your plants have plenty of space to grow. Finally, ensure that it is safe to dig in your garden and you're not going to dig up any pipes or wires that could be dangerous. Raised bed gardens have the same requirements in terms of sunlight, ease of watering, and so on as in-ground gardens.

2. Evaluate sun requirements and exposure: Most vegetables need at least 6–8 hours of direct sunlight per day, and ideally 8–10 hours. Some leafy greens like a bit more shade. Check seed packets or plants' labels/instructions for their sun requirements. Create a sun map for your garden (for relevant areas of your garden that you want to plant in) and measure the full sun, filtered/part shade, and full shade. Do this over the year to see how it

differs with the seasons. Ideally, this should be done for every hour throughout the day, but every 2 hours also works. If you don't want to do a sun map, you could consider getting a garden light meter or a time-lapse camera instead.

3. When to plant: Typically, you would need to wait after the last frost before planting your garden. Check the seed packets or plant tags. Check the soil temperature—it should be 60–85°F (15–30°C). Most seeds won't germinate if the soil temperature is below 50°F (10°C). You can start seeds indoors before the last frost to get a head start on the growing season and transplant the seedlings outside when they are ready. You can do succession planting by planting hardy crops first, such as broccoli, peas, garlic, onions, cabbage, then half-hardy crops, such as carrots, potatoes, and lettuce, and then tender crops, such as beans, corn, peppers, and tomatoes.

The next chapter will look at starting your garden, covering both starting a no-till garden from scratch as well as transitioning to no-till if you have an existing garden. It will also cover building raised beds in case you'd prefer to go this route.

Chapter 3: Starting Your Garden

Starting a garden is super exciting! By now you have a good understanding of what no-till gardening is about, and you'll have given thought as to the best location for your garden, thinking about the sun requirements and exposure and many other factors, like ease of access, watering, any areas of shade, shelter from the elements, and so on. You will have given thought to the time of year you want to start your garden and which plants are best suited for growing in your area.

This chapter is moving on to the really practical hands-on part of starting your garden from scratch or transitioning to no-till if you have a garden already. This chapter will cover how you start no-till garden beds from scratch and how you can transition your existing garden to no-till as well. It will also cover building raised beds.

Starting from Scratch

There is a variety of methods you can use to start a no-till garden from scratch, such as the no-dig gardening method, lasagna gardening, hugelkultur, and others. They do have a lot in common, though. Most no-till gardening methods recommend just covering the area with cardboard and/or newspapers and building garden beds on top of it by layering organic materials, such as compost, hay, kitchen scraps, and more. This works really well even if you have not so great soil, plus it allows you to have great results rather quickly—you can usually start planting right after setting up your garden beds, and the cardboard or newspapers will decompose by the time the plants' roots reach it.

However, these methods do have their cost. You will need quite a bit of organic matter, including compost, straw, and kitchen scraps, plus you will have to bring them in to your garden beds. With that said, making your own compost is not difficult at all, and it will be covered in detail in Chapter 6. Not only will it help you build your soil, but it also uses things you usually throw away in the trash, so it's a win-win situation.

The no-dig method is about trying not to disturb the soil at all or keep the disturbance to a minimum and leaving things like organic matter on the surface of the soil. The organic matter feeds the soil (which is what happens in nature) and helps with drainage and aeration. In nature, leaves fall off trees onto the ground, and bacteria and fungi attack them and turn them into natural compost. Then creatures like earthworms and beetles carry the decomposed material deeper into the soil where plants' roots can use the nutrients.

Personally, I prefer using the no-dig method to start no-till garden beds. It is suited to all types of soil, even heavy clay. The soil stays healthy because it's not disturbed, and you get healthier, stronger plants. You don't use a fork or a spade to loosen or dig the soil, so you don't disturb the microorganisms, the fungi, and the worms in it. Your soil will retain more moisture, and you'll get fewer weeds. You will also end up using less fertilizers and pesticides. Plus, you won't get backache or blisters on your hands from needing to dig the soil.

With the no-dig gardening method, you simply enrich your soil by adding compost as well as nitrogen- and carbon-rich materials to it. These layers break down to create a fantastic growing environment for your plants. The no-dig method is an organic gardening approach that emulates nature, and it can be used in gardens of any size. The first year that you do no-dig may be the most demanding because you may need to prepare your garden beds, which includes removing rocks, grass, and weeds and adding compost and organic matter, but I promise it does get easier ever after and is definitely worth it in the long run.

How to Start a No-Till Garden Bed

Charles Dowding was the person who first started the no-dig method, and he suggests initially starting out with a small area of 4 by 8 feet (1.2 by 2.4 m). He states that you can get just as good a harvest from this area as a larger area, and he uses a space like this to do succession planting all year long. He suggests that you choose a space for your no-dig garden beds away from tall trees and hedges because they take moisture from the soil and create shade, and shady areas also host slugs. In Dowding's vast experience, he has found that using the no-dig method results in much better harvests than when you cultivate your soil. You can start a no-dig bed by layering compostable materials like a lasagna.

Here's how you start a no-till garden bed using the no-dig method:

1. Prepare the Area and Cover It in Light-Blocking Material

To start a no-till garden bed, you need to remove rocks and weeds first. Remove the rocks, cut the weeds at the ground level, and add them to your compost pile. Then use cardboard or newspapers to block out the sunlight so that weeds can't continue to grow. Make sure to overlap sheets of cardboard or newspaper so that no light gets through. If you're using newspapers, lay down a thick layer with 6–10 sheets. Water the cardboard or newspapers—this will help them conform to the ground better and will keep them from being blown away by wind.

2. Add Layers

After this, you can add an optional thin 1-inch (2.5 cm) layer of kitchen scraps, consisting of fruit and vegetable peels or waste, tea bags, coffee grounds, eggshells, and so on. Then you need to add a 2-inch (5 cm) layer of compost or manure, then a 3–4-inch (7.5–10 cm) layer of straw, then another 2-inch (5 cm) layer of compost or manure, and then a final 3–4-inch (7.5–10 cm) layer of straw. It's sensible to water each layer well before adding the next layer. Your bed will compact as you water it. Aim to have it at least 6 inches (15 cm) tall after watering. You can continue layering it and have it taller than that if you'd like. Here are the layers of a no-dig garden bed in order:

1) Light-blocking material, like cardboard or newspapers
2) Kitchen scraps and food waste
3) Compost, manure, or a mix of both
4) Straw
5) Compost, manure, or a mix of both
6) Straw

You can add temporary wooden sides to your beds, and these will help keep your beds in shape for the first few months. This is not necessary, though. It's quicker and cheaper to make open-sided beds, and they will have fewer hiding places for slugs, ants, and woodlice. However, you must have weed-free paths between beds for this to work and absolutely no grass, which otherwise would invade beds with no sides.

If you have a lot of compost, the easiest way to create garden paths is to mulch them with compost. You can cover your whole garden area with cardboard or newspapers in order to prevent weeds and grass from growing, then you can create your garden beds, and then you need to simply mulch the garden paths between them with compost. You would need a 2-inch (5 cm) layer of compost for garden paths.

If you don't have a lot of compost, you can use other materials, like wood chips. Wood chips are cheap, and they break down with time, enriching your soil with nutrients. You need at least a 1-inch (2.5 cm) layer of wood chips, although I would suggest making it 2 inches (5 cm). You'll need to replace or top up the wood chips every few years.

3. Make Holes for Planting

Once you have these layers, you can create little indentations of 4 inches (10 cm) into the top layer of straw, fill them with compost, and then plant seeds or seedlings in there. By having these layers, you are creating the best growing medium for your plants as your plants are growing.

It's good to have a compost pile so that you have compost when you need it. Making your own compost is not difficult at all, and Chapter 6 has a section dedicated to making and using compost. The height of the original bed you make will shrink down as it breaks down—it will approximately halve in height in the first 6 months as it composts away, but you can add around 2 inches (5 cm) of mulch in the spring and top it up throughout the year to keep the soil full of nutrients.

No-till areas never need tilling or digging in the future, and when other farmers may be suffering with their land due to wet summers, no-till areas will still do well and thrive.

You can plant in no-till garden beds right away. The cardboard will soften within 3 months, and plants will be able to root into the soil. However, it can be a good idea to plant shallow-rooted plants early on so that the cardboard and lower layers have time to decompose before planting deep-rooted plants. Cool-season crops, like lettuce, arugula, and radishes, are perfect for this. Later on, as the layers of materials break down further, you can plant deep-rooted plants, like peas, beans, tomatoes, squash, and more. Peas and beans also help enrich the soil with nitrogen, which will benefit the crops that are planted in later years.

Transitioning to No-Till

If you already have an established garden and would like to transition to no-till, then the process will be slightly different than starting a no-till garden from scratch. In short, you will need to establish permanent garden beds, mow or chop down residues, use a tarp to kill the weeds and/or grass, add some compost to the garden beds, and then lightly hoe or rake them and aerate them with a broadfork. After that, you can start planting in your newly established no-till garden beds right away. With that said, let's take a closer look at each of the steps.

1. Establishing Permanent Garden Beds

Establishing permanent garden beds is the first and most important part of transitioning to no-till. You need to create permanent garden beds where you never walk on the soil for no-till techniques to work properly. Walking or running heavy equipment over your soil compacts it, which in turn causes problems with aeration, waterlogging, and makes the soil hard, which means plants' roots will have a hard time trying to penetrate it. While establishing permanent garden beds will take some time and effort, the good news is that they only need to be established once, and then you'll just need to maintain them.

Mark out your garden beds, and make sure they are no more than 4 feet (1.2 m) wide so that you can reach everywhere without having to step on them. Don't forget to plan for garden paths so that you can walk around your garden without stepping on your garden beds. You can add temporary wooden sides to your beds, and these will help keep your beds in shape for the first few months. This is not necessary, though. It's quicker and cheaper to make open-sided beds, and they will have fewer hiding places for slugs, ants, and woodlice.

2. Removing Residues (But Keeping Roots Intact)

Once your garden beds are laid out, you need to remove any residue that is currently in them. If you have established beds, this usually happens when harvest is complete and you need to "flip" the beds to plant something new. For new garden beds, you may need to use the tarping method in order to smother any grass or weeds, which will be described a bit later.

Keeping the soil covered with mulch and colonized by living roots are key principles of no-till gardening. As long as you don't have any soilborne diseases, like root rot or club root, it's best to leave plants' roots in the soil rather than yank them out. If the growing season is coming to an end and you'd like to start transitioning to no-till, this is what you would want to do. You can do this by simply removing the above-ground part of plants and leaving the roots in the soil to decompose.

Microorganisms in the soil will break down the old crop roots, enriching it with nutrients and leaving many tunnels for water and nutrients to flow through. This will help make your soil fluffier and more aerated and will improve its structure. The old roots also provide a habitat where beneficial microorganisms can live while they wait for new roots to colonize.

When it comes to removing old crops, a lawn mower, a string trimmer, pruners, or loppers are the best tools for removing the above-ground part of old crops without having to yank out whole plants. If you have a lawn mower or a flail mower, you can run it over the bed to chop up the leaves of low-growing crops, such as lettuce, spinach, basil, cilantro, and other greens. This will create a nice layer of decayed leaves that will work as mulch and quickly break down in place, providing nutrients for the next crop. If you don't mind using motorized tools, a string trimmer works great. It's very convenient and will help save your back because you can stand up straight and chop crop residues at ground level, leaving the roots in place.

If you need to kill larger crops, like tomatoes, broccoli, or kale, you can use sharp pruners or loppers to chop them off at the base. You can then add the upper foliage to your compost pile or put it in the trash if there are any signs of diseases. Make sure to leave the roots in any time you need to terminate or remove a crop, for example, when the growing season ends or when cover crops are finished.

3. Killing Weeds and/or Grass Using Tarping

Tarping is a quick and easy method for smothering grass or weeds, and it's great when you need to prepare newly established beds. Not only will it save you back-breaking labor, but it's also perfect for no-till because it doesn't require disturbing the soil.

You simply need to lay a tarp over your bed, and it will block the light to any plants beneath it, killing them without using any chemicals. It also helps warm the soil more quickly in the spring, so you can plant a little bit sooner.

Here is how you kill weeds or grass using the tarping method:

1. First, you'll need thick silage tarps made with garden-safe plastic, like HDPE (high-density polyethylene). Make sure to get black or green tarps so that no light can get through.
2. Now you need to lay the tarps over your garden beds or an area where you'd like to establish new beds. If the weeds or grass are tall, mow or chop them down to 4 inches (10 cm) or less before covering them with the tarps. You should weigh the edges down with bricks, smooth rocks, or sandbags so that no light can get through. Try to make sure nothing sharp touches your tarps so that they don't get cut or damaged.
3. Leave the tarps in place for 1–2 weeks. If you have lots of weeds or grass, you can lift the tarps up and water beneath them to signal the regrowth of existing root systems, then let the area stay exposed for a few days and cover it with the tarps again. Leave for 1 week, and if necessary, repeat the process to exhaust perennial root systems.
4. When you remove the tarps, everything under them should be dead and dry.

This is an easy and convenient method to clear large areas without tillage, which is often used by small-scale no-till farmers. It is also useful if you have lots of perennial weeds or grasses and need to get rid of them. If you till or chop them, you can inadvertently spread them further around your garden. Using tarping helps kill aggressive weeds or grasses and stop them from spreading.

4. Adding Compost

Once your garden beds are prepared and clean on the surface, it's time to nurture your soil. Newly transitioned no-till beds usually need a lot of compost, but you will need much less with time. Initially, I would recommend adding 2–4 inches (5–10 cm) of compost over the surface of your garden beds. In future years, you'll only need 1 or 2 inches (2.5–5 cm) of compost.

If you have a compost pile, I would suggest getting a quality wheelbarrow and a shovel to make moving and spreading compost easier, or you could buy bags of compost that you can dump in place. Your compost should be thoroughly aged, and it should not be hot or steamy, which means the compost is still breaking down. It should have a pleasant, earthy odor, and if there are any putrid or rotting odors, it could mean that the compost may contain pathogens. If that's the case, you'll need to mix the compost with more carbon-rich materials, like straw or wood chips, and let it break down further before adding it to the garden.

5. Smoothing the Beds Using a Rake or a Hoe

A rake or a hoe are great tools to smooth the upper layer of your beds in order to prepare them for planting. It helps spread the compost without breaking up the chunks. Some pressure from your rake or hoe is fine, but try not to chop the compost up too much.

If you are used to regular tillage-based gardening methods, you may be tempted to mix the compost into the soil, but you shouldn't do it. The compost should stay on the surface of your garden beds in order to minimize disturbance. Soil organisms will incorporate the organic matter with time.

Worms will come up and grab little pieces of compost and will then take them deeper into the soil. Water will also penetrate the compost and help carry it down over time.

6. Aerating the Soil with a Broadfork

A broadfork or a digging fork are great tools for no-till growers. The long tines of these tools help deeply aerate your soil without damaging its structure, flipping over the layers, or disturbing microorganisms. When the tines go into the soil, they add oxygen and air pockets. They also create channels for organic matter to seep deeper, so you don't have to blend it in.

Using a broadfork is rather simple—you just need to drop it in, step on the horizontal bar, and lightly pull backward on the handles to lift the tines upward. Then, you simply move the broad fork back about a foot (30 cm) and repeat the process. If you have compacted soil, you should get a 14-16-inch-deep (35–40 cm) broadfork. If you have relatively loose soil or raised beds, then 10–12-inch-long (25–30 cm) tines are just fine.

In the first couple of years after transitioning to no-till, you may need to use the broadfork several times to break up soil compaction. With time, as the soil becomes looser and healthier, you won't have to use it anymore.

You can use the broadfork before or after raking—this depends on your planting schedule. If you're sowing directly, I would recommend a light raking after using the broadfork. If you are transplanting seedlings, you can plant them right after broadforking so that the new plants can penetrate their roots into the bed more easily.

7. Planting Your Newly Established Garden Beds

Planting in no-till beds is essentially the same as your standard planting process. You can get a dibber to make planting a bit easier—it's an excellent tool for making planting holes. You simply need to put some weight on it, and you'll make a nice gap for your transplants—it's really easy to pop in your plants this way.

Once the growing season is over, you should maintain constant soil coverage in no-till garden beds. If you aren't growing a new crop of vegetables or fruits, you can sow cover crops or deeply mulch the bed to protect the soil until you are ready to use it again.

Starting a Raised Bed Garden

If you'd like to start a raised bed garden and you're wondering what kind of wood you should use to build your raised beds, how large a raised bed should be, or how to clear a site and build a bed, this section of the book will help you.

A raised bed is essentially a frame box that has no top or bottom. It's usually raised above the ground in a sunny spot. You can build a raised bed without a frame—it can be a mound of soil—but I personally prefer framed raised beds to keep everything in place and stop the sides from crumbling and expanding.

Raised beds have quite a few benefits. They drain well and help prevent soil erosion. They also warm up more quickly in the springtime than the soil in your garden does. You have control over the soil you place in raised beds. Raised beds aren't as prone to weeds because they are elevated and you can fill them with weed-free soil. They also make tending to your garden more convenient because you don't have to bend down so far, so they are great for people with mobility issues. If you only have a small space, raised beds could be a great solution for you.

Raised beds can look attractive and neat too. Having raised beds makes it very easy to separate and rotate crops. Raised beds are great for no-till gardening. The minimum size for a raised bed is usually 4x4 feet (1.2x1.2 m), and they should be a minimum of 6 inches (15 cm) tall, but they'll need to be taller for plants that have a deeper root structure—18 inches (45 cm) is usually enough for most plants.

You can make raised beds using anything you have on hand: wood, stones, bricks, or cement blocks. Avoid treated wood because chemicals from it could leach into your soil. If you choose pine, it is inexpensive but may rot after a few years. You can get rot-resistant wood, like cedar or redwood, but it's more expensive. You can also use railroad ties or pallets. Concrete may increase the pH of the soil over time. Cinder blocks are a great material for building raised beds and will retain heat too. Rocks and stones work too, and they look great.

Raised beds should not be wider than 4 feet (1.2 m) so that you can easily reach everywhere without having to step on them. If you're putting a raised bed against a fence or a wall, you might want it to be only 2–3 feet (60–90 cm) wide since you can only access it from one side. Length is not as important. You can make a bed that is 4x4 feet (1.2x1.2 m), or 4x8 feet (1.2x2.4 m), or 4x12 feet (1.2x3.6 m). It can be as long as you want, but I personally find it easier to have multiple shorter beds rather than one really long bed.

How deep your raised beds should be depends on what plants you want to grow. Shallow-rooted plants, such as lettuce, leafy greens, spinach, onions, leeks, basil, chives, radishes, strawberries, chives, dill, mint, cilantro (coriander), parsley, thyme, oregano, and marigolds, need a minimum soil depth of 6 inches (15 cm). Deep-rooted crops, such as carrots, parsnips, beans, beets, broccoli, Brussels sprouts, cabbage, cauliflower, cucumbers, melons, garlic, kale, Swiss chard, turnips, potatoes, squash, rosemary, sage, borage, lavender, calendula, nasturtiums, snapdragons, and sweet alyssum, need a minimum soil depth of 12 to 18 inches (30–45 cm). If you want to grow peppers, tomatoes, okra, eggplants, pumpkins, watermelons, or winter squash, they need the soil to have a depth of 18 inches (45 cm). If plants don't have loose soil to this depth, the roots won't be able to go down deep enough to access nutrients.

Usually, lumber comes in a standard size that is 6 inches (15 cm) in height. You can stack several boards to make your beds 12 or 18 inches (30 or 45 cm) tall or even taller. But keep in mind that the added weight of the soil will add pressure to the sides. You'll need to add cross-supports to any bed that is over 12 inches (30 cm) tall.

You'll need to prepare the area where you plan to build a raised bed before building it. Here's what basic site preparation for a raised bed looks like. First, outline the spot where you plant to build your raised bed. If you have grass in the area, mow it short, and dig out the clumps. Loosen the soil in the bed, flip the clumps of sod upside down, and add them to the bed. You can also scrape the soil from the pathway around the outside and add that to the bed.

You can also use the no-dig method to build raised beds, which I personally prefer. Mow the grass or weeds as close to the ground as possible. Then cover the area with cardboard or newspapers, which will smother the grass and weeds and eventually rot down into the soil as well. Be sure to overlap the cardboard or newspapers by about 6 inches (15 cm) to make sure no weeds slip through cracks. Next, add 6 inches (15 cm) of compost on top of the cardboard. If your raised bed will be 6 inches (15 cm) tall, the compost will be your growing medium. But if it will be taller, you'll need to fill the bed with topsoil and other materials, and the compost will go on top of that.

You can plant your raised beds right after setting them up. By the time the roots reach the cardboard, it will have started to break down, and the roots will be able to grow deeper below that cardboard layer. You can top up your raised beds with an inch or two (2.5–5 cm) of compost each fall or winter. This will help improve the quality and fertility of the soil not only in your raised beds but below them too.

How to Build a Raised Bed

Building a raised is not difficult at all and requires minimal DIY skills. You are essentially building a box with no top and bottom. Most lumber stores can cut the planks for you. Here's what you'll need to build a raised bed:

Tools

- Drill/driver and bits
- Screwdriver
- Hand saw and tape measure if cutting the planks yourself

Materials

- For a 4x8-foot (1.2x2.4 m) bed, get 3 pieces of 8-foot (2.4 m) long 2x6 in. (5x15 cm) lumber. If they have 2x8 in. (5x20 cm) or 2x10 in. (5x25 cm) lumber, that's even better. For a 4x4-foot (1.2x1.2 m) bed, get 2 pieces of lumber. This will make 6-inch-tall (15 cm) beds if you get 2x6 in. (5x15 cm) planks. If you want a taller bed, you'll need to double the amount of planks for a 12-inch-tall (30 cm) bed and triple it for an 18-inch-tall (45 cm) bed.
- You can get pine stakes for extra bracing.
- If you don't have a saw, ask the guys at the lumber yard to cut the pieces in half. For a 4x8-foot (1.2x2.4 m) bed, cut one of the pieces in half, which will give you two 4-foot (1.2 m) lengths to use for the ends. For a 4x4-foot (1.2x1.2 m) bed, cut both pieces in half.

Deck/Exterior Screws

To make your bed stronger, use a piece of 2x4 in. (5x10 cm) or 4x4 in. (10x10 cm) lumber in the corners to give you something stable to nail or screw into rather than the end grain of the board.

And here's how you build your raised bed:

1. If your 8-foot-long (2.4 m) boards were not pre-cut at the lumber store, mark off the half way point, and cut as many planks as you need for the 4-foot (1.2 m) sides of the bed.

2. Screw the planks together using decking screws. Two holes at the end of each plank is enough. Drill pilot holes using a drill bit slightly thinner than the screws themselves. One end of each plank will overlap the end of the next and screw directly into it, so position your pilot holes correspondingly. It will be easier if you have a helper to hold it while you fasten the corners.

3. If you'd like extra bracing and a sturdier frame, cut your pine stake into 4 pieces, and use them to nail the boards at the corners for bracing.

4. With all the wood cut to size and the holes drilled, you can start putting the bed together.

5. Lay down the beds. The walls need to be laid out so that each plank overlaps the next with the pilot holes located at the overlapping end.

6. Screw the walls together with long screws so that each wall is properly secured to the next.

7. Congratulations, you've just built your raised bed, and it's ready to be filled!

You could decide to bury the base of your raised bed slightly to stop weeds from encroaching. You can make your raised bed last longer by putting a heavy plastic liner inside the boards. You could put hardware cloth at the base of your raised beds if you're putting them on soil to prevent things like gophers and moles from getting into your raised beds.

Now it's time to fill your raised beds. If you opted for the no-dig method and your beds are 6 inches (15 cm) tall, you can fill them with compost and use it as the growing medium. If your beds are taller, you'll need to fill them with other materials.[2]

You can fill your raised beds with topsoil and then top it off with 6 inches (15 cm) of compost. If you want to know how much soil your raised beds require, you can use the formula of length x width x depth, and this will give you how much soil you need in cubic feet or cubic meters.

Apart from just topsoil and compost, you can add things like vermiculite, worm castings, coconut coir, peat moss, and grass clippings. Below you will find a recipe for mixing soil for raised beds. I've been using it for years, and we've gotten some of the best harvests using this mix. It's a bit more complicated but definitely worth it. The amounts are for one 4x4-foot (1.2x1.2 m) raised bed. You can multiply the amounts for larger beds.

- 4 cubic feet (113 L) of topsoil
- 3 cubic feet (85 L) of coconut coir (you can use peat moss instead)
- 2–3 cubic feet (56.5–85L) of compost or composted manure
- 2-inch (5 cm) layer of shredded leaves or grass clippings

---

[2] Image from https://www.almanac.com/content/how-build-raised-garden-bed

If you use grass clippings, make sure they are not from a lawn that has been sprayed with herbicides or been fertilized with food that contains granular herbicides to kill weeds. They both persist and will kill plants up to 3 years after the initial application. Simply mix all the materials with a hoe or a cultivator and water well. Now you're ready to fill your raised beds. If you use this recipe, you probably won't need to fertilize your raised beds much in the first year. But in the following years, you can add an inch or two (2.5–5 cm) of compost.

Checking and Changing Soil pH Level

You can get soil tests done where you check the pH level of your soil to see if it is acidic or alkaline. You can purchase pH testing kits online or at your local garden center. The instructions are easy to follow, and you will likely have to mix a sample of your soil with water and other ingredients and then dip a test strip in the solution. If the pH level is outside of the range, you may need to adjust it by using amendments.

The pH scale ranges from 0 to 14. The lower end of the scale is acidic, and the higher end is alkaline. The middle point—7.0—is neutral. Most plants prefer to grow in soil with a pH level between 6.0 and 7.5. Few plants, such as blueberries, need acidic soil with a pH level between 4 and 5.5.

You can use sulfur or aluminum sulfate to lower the pH level of your soil (make it more acidic). You can also use peat moss or fresh pine needles to make your soil more acidic, but these are usually not as effective and don't work as quickly as sulfur or aluminum sulfate. To increase the pH level of your soil (make it less acidic), you can add finely ground agricultural limestone. The amounts of sulfur, aluminum sulfate, or lime should be carefully measured before adding, so I would suggest checking with your local garden center—they should be able to help you with that.

I remember when I first started implementing no-till methods in my garden. I chose a sunny area in the garden and started preparing my no-till garden beds by putting down cardboard on the grass, then compost, vegetable scraps, straw, more compost, and more straw. I made indentations in it, filled them with compost, and planted seedlings in there that I had grown from seed indoors 8 weeks earlier. We also had raised beds in a different part of our garden that had potatoes growing in them. I had tomatoes growing in the no-till area of my garden, and I didn't want to plant potatoes near them because potatoes and tomatoes can be attacked by the same blight. The raised beds worked perfectly for that, and we had an abundant crop of both tomatoes and potatoes that year.

Key takeaways from this chapter:

1. No-till gardening aims to keep soil disturbance to a minimum, like in nature. It relies on using organic matter to feed the soil and help with drainage and aeration. It is easier for you and better for the environment. If you're starting from scratch, you can layer cardboard, newspapers, scraps, straw, and compost or manure when making no-till garden beds.

2. If you already have an existing garden and would like to transition to no-till, you'll have to establish permanent garden beds, mow or chop down residues, use a tarp to kill the weeds and/or grass, add some compost to the garden beds, and then lightly

hoe or rake them and aerate them with a broadfork. After that, you can start planting in your newly established no-till garden beds right away.

3. Raised beds are a great choice for no-till gardening. With raised beds, you can choose what soil to put in there. There will be no soil compaction. You won't have to bend or kneel. They need to be at least 6 inches (15 cm) tall, but they can be up to 18 inches (45 cm) tall for plants that have deeper roots. You can put hardware cloth at the bottom of raised beds to prevent moles and gophers from getting into your raised beds.

4. You can get soil tests done where you check the pH level of your soil and then adjust it if necessary. You can use sulfur or aluminum sulfate to lower the pH level of your soil (make it more acidic). To increase the pH level of your soil (make it less acidic), you can add finely ground agricultural limestone. The amounts of sulfur, aluminum sulfate, or lime should be carefully measured before adding, so I would suggest checking with your local garden center—they should be able to help you with that.

The next chapter will look at seeding and transplanting, and it will cover selecting and germinating seeds as well as transplanting your seedlings into bigger pots and eventually outdoors to grow and thrive. It will also cover propagating plants from cuttings, which allows you to clone existing plants.

Chapter 4: Seeding and Transplanting

This chapter will cover everything you need to know about seeding and transplanting. Now that you have prepared your no-till garden beds, it's time to move on to planting them with lovely vegetables that will produce an abundance of delicious produce for you and your family.

This chapter will cover how you select and start seeds and how you grow and transplant seedlings. Planting a garden is one of my favorite parts of gardening, and I never cease to be amazed at what wonderful things you can grow from seeds. It's enormously satisfying checking on your seeds progress daily and watching them transform first into seedlings, then into plants, and finally see them produce delicious vegetables that can feed you and your family and friends. All home-grown organically and naturally without any chemicals, by you!

Selecting and Starting Seeds

Gardening would be super expensive if you were to buy all your plants as already established. Generally, the more established a plant is, the more expensive it is to buy because of all the work that has gone into getting it to that state. It is much cheaper to grow your own plants from seed. Growing plants from seed is not difficult, and it's so rewarding and enjoyable to see your plants grow from seed to finally gathering harvest from them. I can still remember the very first time I grew tomatoes from seed. Checking on their progress is one of the first things I did every day, and I bored my family and friends with constant updates on how they did, but I was so proud and excited to have grown actual plants from seed.

Ensure that you buy your seeds from a reputable company. I strongly suggest getting organic seeds. Organic seeds are seeds taken from plants grown without the use of synthetic fertilizers and pesticides, which means they are better for you and for the environment. Plants grown from organic seeds are also naturally better at fending off pests on their own.

Check the seed packet to see if the plants you want to grow would grow well in your location. You could look for regionally based companies with seeds that thrive in your area. Regional suppliers are less likely to offer seeds that are unsuited to your growing conditions.

When you are choosing vegetables to plant, do look on the back of seed packets or in the seed catalog for seeds that have characteristics of being disease resistant because this will give you better quality vegetables and may reduce pests that come into your garden. While you can keep seeds for a few years, it is preferable to buy new seeds each year to ensure you get a better crop.

Also, check the seed packet for details about the best time to sow them and what conditions the plants like to grow in. Most seed packets will tell you if they should be started indoors or sown directly in the garden. They will usually tell you how long it will take for the plants to produce edible produce (days to maturity), and they should tell you their light and water requirements. Some may give information about the type of soil the plant likes.

Make a list of the vegetables and herbs that you enjoy eating, and then think about where these would grow in your garden. If you're a complete beginner to gardening, I would suggest starting out with vegetables that are easy to grow. Lettuce, green beans, peas, radishes, carrots, cucumbers, kale, Swiss chard, beets, and zucchini are all relatively easy to grow. Tomatoes and peppers require a bit more care, but they are not terribly difficult to grow. Eggplants, cauliflower, celery, and watermelons can be more difficult to grow.

If you don't like certain vegetables, don't grow them because if you don't enjoy eating them—it'll probably be just wasted time and food unless you plan to sell them. Remember that if you're growing peas, pole beans, cucumbers, tomatoes, or other vining plants, you'll need to have trellises to support them when they grow, and also remember that they may create shade as they grow, so take this into consideration. If you're planting pumpkins and watermelons, they need a lot of space to spread.

You can start seeds indoors—usually before the last frost—so that your seedlings are ready to be transplanted outside to the garden when the weather is warmer. Seed packets may say things like "plant inside 6 to 8 weeks before last frost". You would typically start seeds in a seed starting tray or in small containers and then transplant the seedlings into bigger containers when they grow too big before finally transplanting them to your garden.

Some plants can be started indoors and then be transplanted outside. Plants that can be started indoors include artichoke, basil, broccoli, Brussels sprouts, cabbage, cauliflower, celery, chard, chives, collard greens, eggplants, kale, leeks, mustard, parsley, peppers, and tomatoes.

Some plants don't transplant well and should be planted directly into the soil (this is called direct sowing). Plants that should be started directly in the soil include beans, beets, carrots, corn, garlic, okra, parsnips, pumpkins, radishes, squash, turnips, watermelons, and zucchini.

Some vegetables are grown from root divisions or bulbs. Some examples include asparagus, garlic, horseradish, onions, potatoes, rhubarb, and sweet potatoes. This will be covered in more detail in Chapter 9 in individual plant profiles.

You can grow seeds in any containers, and this could be a good way to recycle butter or margarine tubs or yogurt pots. The container needs to be 2–3 inches (5–7.5 cm) deep with some drainage—you can simply poke a drainage hole at the bottom. You can also purchase seed starting trays especially for this purpose, and it does make transplanting seedlings easier when you need to.

You can start seeds in potting mix, but most seeds, especially smaller ones, do better when started in seed starting mix, and it should be a fresh, sterile mix. I would advise against starting seeds in potting soil and especially in garden soil because this can lead to fungal diseases and kill your seeds. Seed starting mix is a special form of soilless potting mix that typically uses smaller particles of vermiculite and sand and omits organic materials found in standard potting soil. You can loosen and dampen the seed starting mix before planting seeds, but don't soak it. If you start seeds in seed starting mix, you'll generally need to transplant the seedlings into a standard potting mix or potting soil when they begin to develop into larger plants.

You can make your own seed starting mix by mixing equal parts of coco coir, perlite, and vermiculite. Simply combine all the ingredients in a clean tub or bucket, and water the mixture well. Stir the mixture with your hands or a trowel until it's moist but not soggy (like a wrung-out sponge). You can fill your seed starting trays or pots with this mix and sow your seeds right away.

You can also make your own potting mix for transplanting your seedlings into when they grow. You can make a basic potting mix or an enriched one with compost. To make a basic potting mix, mix 6 parts coco coir, 1 part perlite, and 1 part vermiculite. Enriched potting mix is made by mixing 4 parts coco coir, 2 parts compost, 1 part perlite, and 1 part vermiculite. Simply combine all the ingredients in a clean tub or bucket, and water the mixture well. Then stir it until it's moist but not soggy.

Look at the packet instructions diligently for how deep you should plant your seeds. Some small seeds just need to be scattered over the surface of the soil, while others need to be planted in a hole. If you don't have a dibber (a tool for making holes to plant seeds into), you can simply use an old pencil to make a hole, drop the seed in, and then cover it with soil if you're sowing directly or seed starting mix if you're starting seeds indoors. It's a good idea to plant 2–3 seeds per hole because not every seed you plant will germinate. There isn't anything you're doing wrong—it's just nature.

If more than one seed grows, you can thin them out. It simply means you should let the strongest looking one grow and cut the rest at the base. You should thin out seedlings when they have developed 1–2 true leaves. The very first leaves that plants grow from seed are called seed leaves or cotyledons. They are long and narrow in some plants, but in others, they are heart shaped. True leaves come after seed leaves. They have the same shape as the adult foliage, just baby sized.

You will need to keep the soil or seed starting mix moist but not soggy. You would typically need to water your seeds daily, and you can spray your seed starting mix with a spray bottle if you're starting seeds indoors, or you can spray the soil with a fine spray hose nozzle or water it with a watering can if you're direct sowing seeds in the garden.

If you're starting seeds indoors, you can keep the seeds covered with a clear plastic dome or wrap, and this will help them to germinate more quickly. You can purchase heating mats to germinate seeds because most seeds germinate well in temperatures between 65 and 75°F (18–24°C). Your seeds will need to be watered more if you use a heating mat. You could also place a fan near them to improve air circulation.

Once the seedlings emerge, remove the plastic dome or wrap you had covering them. When the seedlings have started to grow, keep watering them the same way. Keep the soil or seed starting mix moist but not soggy—it should feel like a damp sponge. You would typically need to water your seedlings daily.

If you're starting seeds indoors, put the tray in a place where your seedlings will receive lots of sunlight. If they're too far away from light once they've germinated, they'll start to get long and leggy because they reach for the light, but this will make them weaker. The only way to prevent seedlings from becoming leggy is to provide more light. You can do that by getting grow lights for your seedlings.

Having adequate lighting is essential for growing seedlings successfully. When I was just starting out with gardening decades ago, I tried starting plants from seed indoors without artificial lighting. I was lucky to have a massive south-facing window in my living room, and that's where I first tried starting seeds. That worked okay, but my seedlings were thin and leggy, especially compared to the ones you'd find in a garden center. Also, at least half of the seeds didn't sprout at all. And things got only worse when I tried starting different plants from seed. It was clear that they didn't get enough light from my large windowsill. That's when I decided to splurge on grow lights, and I was amazed at the difference it made! Almost all of my seeds started sprouting, and the seedlings became much stronger and healthier, and they had no problem surviving the transition to my in-ground garden, raised beds, containers, and even hydroponic systems.

You would typically use fluorescent or LED (light-emitting diode) grow lights for starting seeds. Metal halide (MH) and high-pressure sodium (HPS) lights produce lots of heat and can burn seedlings. Fluorescent grow lights are cheaper than LEDs; however, LED grow lights have a few benefits over fluorescent grow lights. They are more energy efficient and last longer than fluorescent grow lights. They also don't lose their effectiveness over time.

If you get grow lights for seedlings, you shouldn't leave them on all day long. Seedlings need 14–16 hours of light per day, so you should have your lights on a timer for convenience. Some people grow seedlings with 12 hours of light daily, but it's usually not enough in my experience. You can try that, but you should monitor your seedlings closely in this case. If they start getting tall and growing sideways, you should add 2 more hours of light per day.

How high you should have grow lights above your seedlings depends on the type of lights you have. I'd suggest following the height recommendations provided by the light manufacturer. However, if that information isn't provided, fluorescent grow lights should be kept 2–3 inches (5–7.5 cm) above seedlings, and LED grow lights should be at least a foot (30 cm) above. You'll need to move your grow lights away from the seedlings as they grow.

Issues with Seeds

If not all your seeds germinate, it's worth having another read of the back of the seed packet to see if you did everything it suggested in terms of temperature, light, and water. Have the seeds rotted because the soil was too moist? Or was the soil too dry, and the seeds dried out? Try again and try to follow the instructions and be consistent with how moist your soil is.

If your seedlings are tall, leggy, and spindly, it could be that they aren't getting enough light, so they're growing to try to reach the light. They should get 14–16 hours of bright light per day, which you can help along with grow lights. If the temperature is too warm, this can cause plants to be leggy too. If that's the case, you could reduce the temperature in the room and also use a little less fertilizer.

In the picture on the next page, it shows the difference between the seeds on the left, which were grown under grow lights, and the seeds on the right, which were grown on a windowsill and have become leggy.[3]

If your seedlings looked good, and then suddenly they toppled at the base, this could be due to a soil-borne fungus known as damping off. Damping off can affect most seedlings, particularly under conditions of high humidity, poor air circulation, and if seeds were sown too thickly. It is mainly a problem when starting seeds indoors. Damping off is mainly caused by overly moist soil, which is ideal for the growth and spread of fungal pathogens.

There is no cure for plants that have damping off. If you have it in the soil, I would recommend getting rid of it and using a soilless growing medium instead because you can't get rid of it once it's there. This is why I recommend using seed starting mix, which is a soilless growing medium, for starting seeds in the first place. Also, try not to overwater your seed starting mix and sow the seeds more thinly because overcrowding can lead to damping off.

When I first tried to grow cucamelon seeds, I had this happen, and it was so frustrating to see little seeds starting to sprout and then just die for what seemed like no good reason. I then started using seed starting mix to start seeds and never had this problem again.

If you have mold growing on the surface of the seed starting mix or potting mix, this is a sign that the growing medium is too wet. It may not harm the plants too much, but definitely stop watering them for a few days, and you could put a fan nearby too, which will help with air circulation. You can scrape off the mold or put the seedlings in fresh potting mix, but be really careful and try not to damage them.[4]

Growing and Transplanting Seedlings

When you're growing seedlings, the growing medium needs to be kept moist but not soggy. The best indicator that your seeds or seedlings need water is how dry their growing medium is. When you touch the potting mix or soil, it should feel neither soggy nor too dry. Instead, it should feel like a moist sponge. When watering your seedlings, use a mister or a very gentle spray bottle to water the top of your seed starting tray or container. If you sowed seeds directly, you can water your seedlings carefully with a fine spray hose nozzle or a watering can.

---

[3] Image from https://www.gardeners.com/how-to/how-to-start-seeds/5062.html

[4] Image from https://www.thespruce.com/successful-start-seed-indoors-1402478

If you have grow lights, remember to raise them as the seedlings grow so that you don't burn them. You could also have a fan in the room to keep air circulating well. You should fertilize seedlings with an organic liquid fertilizer when they grow to 3 inches (7.5 cm) and then weekly after that.

One of the best ways to determine if a seedling is ready to be transplanted outside is to look at how many true leaves it has. The very first leaves that plants grow from seed are called seed leaves or cotyledons. They are long and narrow in some plants, but in others, they are heart shaped. True leaves come after seed leaves. They have the same shape as the adult foliage, just baby sized. You will need to wait until your seedlings have at least 3–4 true leaves before transplanting them to your garden.

However, if the weather is still too cold, you can continue growing seedlings indoors. You will have to pot them up as they grow, though. Potting up seedlings, whether you've grown them yourself or have purchased them from a nursery, just means putting them into larger containers so that they can grow and thrive. Seedlings need to be put into larger containers so that they have room for their roots to grow and don't become root bound.

If you haven't seen a root-bound plant before, the picture on the right shows what one looks like. This is a tomato seedling that has been in a small container much too long. You can see how the roots have just grown into the container shape because they had nowhere else to go.[5]

You can sometimes gently massage a root-bound plant before you transplant it into a bigger pot, but you need to be careful not to damage the roots when you do this.

When you pot up seedlings, their roots will become bigger and will take up more water. Seedlings are always very thirsty and need lots of water to thrive. When you've put seedlings into their new containers, do remember to feed them because they'll want to take in as many good nutrients as they can to grow strong.

You can plant seedlings when plants are starting to look cramped and overgrown in their small seed starting trays. If plants have started out in 4-inch (10 cm) pots, then around 6–8 weeks after germination they can be moved into 6–8-inch (15–20 cm) pots.

The time for planting seedlings into bigger pots can depend on the plant too. Tomatoes will outgrow their pots very quickly, but herbs can take a bit more time. Tomatoes grow faster than peppers, for example, so they will need to be planted sooner than peppers. Vegetables like squash grow fast and like a lot of

---

[5] Image from https://homesteadandchill.com/potting-up-seedlings/

room, so it can be fine to start squash in 6-inch (15 cm) pots.

If your seedlings are starting to have their roots poke out of drainage holes, this is a key sign that they need to be transplanted into larger containers. You can pot up seedlings before this happens, but this is just a sign they're definitely ready to be put into larger containers.[6]

One helpful tip when you're potting up seedlings is to make a "dummy hole" or placeholder with the existing container in the new container that the seedling is being transplanted into. You can fill the new container with potting soil, then place the existing container in it and check that things are at the right level. Ensure the soil in the new container is moist. When you do this, it will help ensure that there are no air pockets around the plant, and it saves you having to tip in extra soil, which can get all over the leaves of the plant and be a bit awkward. It also means that transplanting of the seedling goes smoothly and stops the plant from being jostled about. Prior to learning about this tip, we often had over- or underfilled containers and had to mess about with soil levels.

When it comes to transplanting seedlings into the garden, don't put them directly outside—the transition to being outside needs to be gradual. You can start by putting them in a protected place outdoors for a few hours while they are still in containers, but bring them back inside at night because it might be too cold for them. Over 10 days, gradually let them get used to being outside more and more. After that, you can transplant them into your garden. A cold frame is also a good place to harden off seedlings.

When you eventually reach the day when you transplant your seedlings into the garden, it could be a good idea to choose an overcast day to reduce the stress for the plants because if they've been indoors or in a greenhouse and then they are placed in the harsh outside world, it can be a shock. Ensure that you water them well, and it can be a good idea to add 2 inches (5 cm) of mulch to keep back the weeds and retain moisture (this will be covered in the next chapter in more detail).

Ensure that there is plenty of space between plants and between rows because plants need room to grow

---

[6] Image from https://homesteadandchill.com/potting-up-seedlings/

and spread out. This will also improve air circulation around the plants, which will help prevent fungal diseases. Crowding plants is a common mistake that gardeners make. If plants are too crowded and don't have enough space between them, it means they will compete for nutrients and space. While seedlings may seem small, they will become much larger as they grow, so do consider the space that mature plants need.

Different plants need different spacing. You can usually find spacing requirements for plants on seed packets. Plant profiles in Chapter 9 will cover spacing requirements for many different plants.

When you come to transplant seedlings, simply poke a hole in the soil, carefully remove the seedling from its container trying not to disturb the roots, put the seedling into the hole you've made, firm the soil around it, and water it thoroughly.

Propagating Plants from Cuttings

If you're just starting out with vegetable gardening, you'll likely have to start plants from seed or purchase seedlings from a nursery. There is another way to start plants, however—from cuttings. It's exactly what it sounds like—you can use cuttings from existing plants to grow new plants. Taking cuttings from plants is a great way to propagate them. It is also called cloning. Some plants can be difficult to start from seed, so you can purchase a plant from a nursery and then propagate it via cuttings.

I have always adored taking plant cuttings. I love the fact that from one plant you can create numerous others and watch them grow. I do this with all my house plants, and I have done this with plants that I grow in my garden too.

When you propagate plants this way, often the plant has done a lot of the growing work, and the new plants grow much quicker than from seed. Only take cuttings from healthy, strong plants. Take a few more cuttings than required because sometimes not all of the cuttings survive.

Here's what you'll need to propagate plants from cuttings:

- Existing plant (parent plant)
- Razor blade or scissors
- Rubbing alcohol
- 4–6-inch (10–15 cm) containers or a seed starting tray
- Clear plastic cover for seed starting tray or a plastic bag
- Soilless potting mix
- Pencil or stick
- Rooting hormone
- Water
- 2 small plastic cups

You'll need a porous, soilless growing medium. You can make your own by mixing equal parts of sand, perlite, peat moss, and vermiculite. Do not add fertilizers or manure to this because they can burn cuttings.

You can start cuttings in seed starting trays, but larger plants may need a 4–6-inch (10–15 cm) deep container. You can also use Styrofoam coffee cups or large paper cups, but make sure to poke a drainage hole at the bottom.

Here's how you propagate plants from cuttings:

1. Choose a healthy parent plant to take cuttings from. Don't take cuttings from diseased or wilting plants. The parent plant should have good, green growth and be large enough to take cuttings from.
2. Next, fill your seed starting tray or container with the growing medium, and poke a hole in it with the pencil.
3. Now you'll need to find suitable stems for cutting. They should be green and non-woody. Newer growth is easier to root than older or woody stems. Find a stem with a node—a bump along the stem where a leaf or a flower bud attaches. New roots will emerge from it.
4. Sterilize your razor blade or scissors with rubbing alcohol, and make a clean cut just below the node. The cutting doesn't need to be long, 4–6 inches (10–15 cm) is enough, but it should have at least 2 leaves and 1 node.
5. Once you've taken the cutting, you need to make a partial slice through the middle of the node with a sterilized razor blade. This will increase the chances of roots emerging from this spot. If your cutting has more than 1 or 2 leaves—cut them off. The cutting only needs 1–2 leaves to continue photosynthesis. Having too many leaves will consume energy that would otherwise go to root creation. If the leaves are very large in relation to the stem, you can cut off the top halves of the leaves too.
6. Next, you'll need to dip the cutting in the rooting hormone. Rooting hormones are typically not organic; however, you can find organic options made with willow extract. I find gel or liquid rooting hormones to be more effective than powder. This step is optional, but rooting hormone can help promote root growth, and I would recommend doing it. Fill one plastic cup with water, and place some rooting hormone into the other one. Dip the node end of the cutting into the water and then into the rooting hormone. Tap off any excess hormone—too much can hinder the chances for successful rooting.
7. Carefully place the cutting into the hole you made in the growing medium, and gently tap the growing medium around the cutting. You can fit several cuttings into one container, but space them out so that the leaves don't touch one another.
8. Place the container with the cutting into a plastic bag, or cover the seed staring tray with a clear plastic cover. It will keep the humidity high and hold in heat. Don't seal the bag completely because cuttings need some airflow to prevent fungal rot. You can remove the cover from the seed starting tray once a day to let the moisture escape. Keep the cuttings in a warm, sunny spot, but don't put them in full sunlight until new leaves start to appear along the stem.
9. Keep the growing medium slightly moist but not so wet that condensation forms on the inside of the plastic bag or seed starting tray cover until the roots form. After 2–3 weeks, you can start checking for roots by tugging gently on the cutting. When you begin to feel resistance, it means the roots have developed. At this point, you can transplant the cutting into your garden or a container.

You can even grow fruit trees from cuttings. The process is essentially the same, but you'll need to take either softwood or semi-hardwood cuttings from branches. Softwood cuttings are generally taken in the spring when new branches are green and no blossoms have appeared. They are flexible but will snap if you bend them hard enough. They dry out pretty quickly, so you'll need to plant them as soon as possible after taking the cuttings. Softwood cuttings usually root in about a month. Semi-hardwood cuttings are harvested in early summer when the new growth is beginning to harden and the green is starting being overtaken by bark. They should still be a little pliable, and they also dry out quickly, so you'll need to plant them as soon as possible. Semi-hardwood cuttings usually root in about 6 weeks.

Cuttings from trees should be between 6 and 12 inches (15–30 cm) long. You'll need to remove leaves from the bottom half of the cutting, and any fruit or buds should be taken off as well. Then you'll need to dip the cut end of the cutting in rooting hormone and plant it just like you would plant a cutting taken from a plant. Once the cuttings have roots that are about 1¼ inches (3 cm), you can transplant them into 4-inch (10 cm) planters. You'll need to grow fruit trees indoors for the first year. You can transplant them into the garden the following spring season. You should slowly harden off your young trees to outdoor conditions before transplanting them into the garden. Of course, it takes years for trees to mature, but if you want to grow a fruit tree from scratch, growing them from cuttings is the best way to go about it. Growing fruit trees from seed can be tricky, and it's much easier to grow them from cuttings.

You can grow a lot of different plants from cuttings, including tomatoes, peppers, celery, sweet potatoes, fennel, basil, rosemary, lemon verbena, lavender, and mint as well as fruit trees, such as lemon, lime, apple, peach, and pear trees, and more.

I remember when I first bought and started seeds for my garden. I sowed carrots and beets directly because they are root crops and don't like being transplanted, and I started tomatoes, basil, and peppers, among other things, indoors because they like warmth and I wanted to get a head start on the growing season by starting them indoors. It's an incredible process all along, from buying packets of seeds at a garden center or online to watching the seeds sprout, grow, and get bigger and stronger, then transplanting the little seedlings into the garden and watching the plants grow, and then eventually seeing these plants flower and fruit. You can hardly believe it—it feels magical.

Key takeaways from this chapter:

1. Seeds are less expensive than seedlings or established plants. Ensure the seeds you use are organic, fresh, and are from a reputable company.
2. Plant seeds for vegetables that you would like to eat and that you know grow well in your area.
3. Use trellises to support climbing or vining plants.
4. Some plants do better when started indoors, whereas some plants don't like to be transplanted and are better sown directly in the garden.
5. You can get disease-resistant seed varieties.
6. You can start seeds indoors before the growing season starts and then transplant them into the garden later in order to get a head start on the growing season.
7. Grow seeds in seed starting mix that is sterile and contains no organic materials to avoid fungal issues.

8. Cover seeds with a plastic dome or plastic wrap. Remove the cover once the seedlings have emerged.
9. You'll need to water your seeds daily and keep the soil or seed starting mix moist but not too wet. Once they sprout, you can water the seedlings daily too. You can give your seedlings liquid fertilizer once they are at least 3 inches (7.5 cm) tall.
10. You can use grow lights to provide more light for your seedlings. Keep them on for 14–16 hours a day on a timer.
11. When seedlings have 3–4 sets of true leaves, they are ready to be transplanted outside. Transition to the outside should be gradual, though. You can move your seedlings outside during the day while they're still in containers, but bring them back inside at night. Do so for 10 days before planting your seedlings outside.
12. Transplant seedlings into your garden on an overcast day so that it is less stressful for them.
13. Give seedlings space and think about their size when they are fully grown.
14. You can also start plants from cuttings (which is also called cloning), and it's a great way to propagate plants.

The next chapter will cover everything you need to know to maintain your garden properly, looking at how to water it and maintenance tasks you need to do to keep your plants healthy and producing a good quality crop and to keep your garden looking its best.

Chapter 5: Maintaining Your Garden

Once you've started your vegetable garden, it does need some care and maintenance to ensure that your plants thrive. You will need to water your plants, keep your garden free from weeds, and mulch the soil to provide nutrients and keep the weeds down. You will also need to prune some plants. It is important to follow the guidance for care on the back of each seed packet. So, this chapter will cover everything you need to know about maintaining your garden.

Watering

How Much You Should Water Your Plants

People can be unsure about how much water they should give their plants and how often they should water them. Watering your garden can depend on the type of soil you have, the climate you live in, the time of year, and the type of plants you are growing.

Having an outside source of water really eases the pressure of having to carry watering cans through your house. And you'll need a lot of watering cans even if you have a small garden. So, if you have access to an outside tap, this is a treasure! If you have a well, you could hook a hose directly to the well for watering. If you don't have an outside tap or a well, you could consider getting a water butt. It's not that expensive, and it will collect lots of delicious rainwater to feed your plants, which they'll love. It would also help you save on your water bill, so it's a win-win situation. If you don't have either of these, you could think about running a hose from a tap in your house out to the garden. Hose reels are very easy to manage. They're convenient and don't take up a lot of space and will make life much easier.

Most plants should ideally get an inch or two (2.5–5 cm) of water each week, and they prefer good, deep watering rather than frequent, shallow watering. When you water more often but not as deeply, you get weak root growth and evaporation. Therefore, watering your garden beds about 1–2 inches (2.5–5 cm) or so once a week is preferable. Most plants typically need 1 inch (2.5 cm) of water per week, although during peak summer you should increase that to 2 inches (5 cm). If it rains, you'll need to water your plants less. To determine when you need to water your plants, you can simply place your finger about an inch (2.5 cm) into the soil, and if it feels dry, you need to water it.

An inch of water is a 1-inch-deep (2.5 cm) layer of water over the entire soil surface in question. Your garden will get some water from rain, so you can make a rain gauge from a straight-sided container, like a used tuna can. Measure 1 and 2 inches (2.5 and 5 cm) up from the bottom, and put lines on the inside at these levels using a permanent marker. Next, add additional marks every quarter of an inch or 5 mm—this will help you determine how much water your garden needs. Place this can on a level spot in the garden where it will be completely exposed to the rain. Check it every week to see how much water your garden got from rain and how much you need to water it. You can purchase a rain gauge from a garden center, but a simple marked container works perfectly fine too.

To measure the volume of water your garden needs, you can simply multiply your garden beds' length by width in inches or centimeters and then by 1 or 2 inches (2.54–5.08 cm, but you can round that up to 2.5–5 cm for convenience) depending on how much water your garden needs. Next, divide the result by 231 if your measurements were in inches and by 1000 if they were in centimeters to get the number of gallons or liters of water your garden needs, respectively. For example, if you have a 4x8-foot garden bed, and your garden needs an inch of water, multiply 48 by 96 by 1, then divide by 231 to determine how many gallons you need. The answer would be 19.95 (you can round that up to 20 for convenience). Or let's say you have a 1.2 by 2.4 m garden bed that needs 2.5 cm of water. You'll need to multiply 120 by 240 by 2.5, then divide by 1000 to determine how many liters you need. In this case, your garden will need 72 liters of water.

When You Should Water Your Plants

First of all, you should water plants once you plant them. For already established gardens, watering them once a week with 1 or 2 inches (2.5–5 cm) of water is OK. However, if the weather is really hot, you may need to water them more frequently—twice a week or even more is the heat scorching. Some vegetables are thirstier and dry out quicker too. In my experience, tomatoes need a lot of water, and their soil can dry out quickly. You can check how moist your soil is by simply placing your finger about an inch (2.5 cm) into the soil. If it feels dry, you need to water it.

When you water your plants, you should aim to water them near the base. Watering your garden in the morning is best unless there has been heavy rain. Plants absorb moisture more effectively in the morning and become hydrated before the weather heats up. If you water your plants in the morning, this allows any water that may get on leaves to dry or evaporate throughout the day rather than just sit there overnight.

If your plants remain wet for extended periods of time, this can lead to fungal diseases. Another thing that can happen if you water your plants in the midday sun and get water on the leaves, the water droplets can act like a magnifying glass and scorch the leaves of your plants.

What Happens if Plants Don't Get Enough Water?

If your plants don't get enough water, this is known as drought stress, and this can cause your plants to produce small fruit or none at all. Vegetables like cabbage and turnips can become tough, bitter, or fibrous. Some may have a flower stalk but then not grow anymore. Or plants could just have wilted leaves, shrivel up, and die.

You can look for signs that plants are underwatered. If they have dry, brown leaf edges, slow leaf growth, leaf curl, yellow leaves, wilted leaves, or branch dieback, these are all signs they may need more water. Don't wait to water your plants if they feel dry, even if the weather forecast says it will rain the next day. If your plants look dry or look like they're suffering from heat, water them. Leafy greens, such as lettuce, kale, and spinach, have shallow root systems and don't hold moisture well, so they do need to be watered regularly to thrive.

What Happens if Plants Get Too Much Water?

It is possible to overwater plants, and this often leads to root rot. Roots need oxygen from the soil, but if it's saturated with water, there's not enough oxygen there. Plants can collapse or have bland fruit if that's the case. If you are growing vegetables with the intention of storing them, they won't store well when it's been really wet—this applies to potatoes, onions, winter squash, and rutabaga.

If plants have any leaf diseases, this will be worse in a wet season. You can't do much if it's rainy, but one solution could be to build raised beds—they offer better drainage because the soil is raised. You can check for signs that a plant is overwatered. If plants look wilted, have brown leaves or yellow falling leaves, if new growth is dropping off, or if a plant is floppy, slimy, or has smelly roots (which is a sign of root rot), this means your plants are likely overwatered.

Drip Irrigation

While watering your plants can be a relaxing experience, it can take quite a bit of time and effort, especially if you have a bigger garden. You can make watering less of a chore by installing a drip irrigation system.

There are different automatic watering systems, like soaker hoses, sprinklers, and drip irrigation systems. Drip irrigation is the most effective way of watering your plants in my opinion. Soaker hoses can often get clogged or crack. Sprinklers can get the leaves wet, and if plants stay wet, they can get fungal diseases. Drip irrigation lines water the soil at an even rate, and you're not wasting water like with sprinklers due to evaporation.

Drip irrigation is a great solution because it helps prevent diseases by minimizing water contact with the leaves, stems, and fruit of plants. It also allows the rows between plants to remain dry, improving access and reducing weed growth. Drip irrigation systems will help you save time, money, and water because they are incredibly efficient.

You can buy drip irrigation kits from garden centers or home improvement/hardware stores. Many kits are modular in design, which allows you to change your drip irrigation system as your garden changes. I would suggest making a plan of your garden and taking it to a store so that they can suggest a kit that would fit your needs best. Drip irrigation kits are relatively affordable and are not very difficult to install, so you can certainly do it yourself, or you can always hire someone to install the system for you.

Watering Raised Beds

You can water your raised beds using a watering can, a garden hose, sprinklers, or drip lines. Watering raised beds with a watering can is very time consuming and can take quite a lot of effort. A garden hose would speed up the process, but don't blast young plants with a hose because this can damage them. You can also place a hose on the soil and let water drain into your raised beds. The soil should never become fully dry in your raised beds. Keep an eye on the weather because your plants may need more (if it's hot) or less water (if it's rainy or cold) as it changes.

Drip Irrigation for Raised Beds

You can get drip irrigation kits for raised beds. Just like with in-ground gardens, this is a great solution for watering your plants. If you have an automatic watering system, it's a good idea to let it water when you are naturally in the garden so that you can check that it's working correctly and there aren't any issues, like a dead battery, a faulty timer, or leaks, and that your raised beds are not being over- or underwatered. Raised beds should be watered evenly and consistently, which is why an automatic watering system can be a good idea. To help retain moisture in your raised beds, you can mulch them, and this will reduce water evaporation and will also help reduce weeds.

Mulching

Mulching means covering the soil with a layer of mulch, which is any material that is spread or laid over the surface of the soil and used for a covering. Mulching helps retain moisture in the soil, reduce weeds, keep the soil and plants' roots cool, and make garden beds and raised beds look more attractive.

You can use different materials for mulching. Some are more aesthetically pleasing than others, while others are more functional and can add nutrients to the soil. There are two categories of mulch: organic and inorganic, and both have their advantages and disadvantages. Organic mulch is made of natural materials. It will decompose over time and add beneficial nutrients to your soil. It can reduce weeds, but it doesn't always fully block weeds. Inorganic mulch is made of synthetic materials. It can fully block weeds, and it's better at retaining moisture than organic mulch, but it won't add nutrients to the soil. No-till gardening uses organic mulch.

Organic mulch materials include compost, shredded leaves, wood chips, pine needles, straw, grass clippings, newspapers, peat moss, and coconut coir. As mentioned previously, organic mulch will decompose, so it will need to be replaced after some time. But while it's decomposing, it will add nutrients to the soil as well as help improve the soil structure, texture, and drainage. The drier and woodier the mulch, the slower it will decompose and the fewer nutrients it will give to the soil.

Wood chips and straw are commonly used for mulching in no-till gardening. These are both great options, as they are relatively affordable and easy to spread. I personally like using compost as mulch. It's one of the best materials for mulching, and it's commonly used with the no-dig method. If you have a compost pile and lots of compost, you can use it for mulching, but wood chips or straw would work just fine too.

If you decide to use pine needles, keep in mind they can reduce the pH level of the soil and make it slightly more acidic, but usually not enough to cause any problems to plants. Also, make sure to use needles that have been dried, or they can rot and cause mold to grow otherwise. Most newspapers should be fine to use for mulching because they use soy-based black inks and hydrogen peroxide for bleaching pulp. But don't use glossy magazines or newspapers with colored or glossy inks because they may contain chemicals that are toxic to plants.

Inorganic mulch materials include plastic or landscape fabric and gravel or stone. Inorganic mulch materials are good at holding in moisture and blocking weeds. Since they don't decompose, they don't add any nutrients to the soil, but at the same time they don't need to be replaced as often as organic mulches.

You can mulch both garden beds and raised beds. Don't add mulch if you've just planted the seeds. The best time to mulch your garden is when the seedlings are at least 3–5 inches (7.5–12.5 cm) tall.

To mulch your garden, simply place your chosen mulch material on the soil, but keep it 3 inches (7.5 cm) away from the base of plants. For trees, leave a 1-foot (30 cm) open ring of space around the tree trunk or 4 to 6 inches (10–15 cm) from each side. Make sure the mulch is dry, and it should be in small pieces. Mulch should be placed on top of the soil but not in it because this will prevent your plants' roots from getting enough water, air, and nutrients they need for healthy growth. You would typically need a 2–3-inch (5–7.5 cm) layer of mulch for it to be effective. Make sure the mulch doesn't touch the leaves of your plants because this can spread diseases.

When you water mulched garden beds or raised beds, aim the water at the base of plants. If you pour water directly on the mulch, it may lead to water retention and root rot. Drip irrigation works great with mulched gardens.

If you're going to grow cover crops, you should remove mulch when the growing season ends. However, if you're not planning to grow cover crops, you should leave it so that it can protect your soil from erosion, plus it will decompose and enrich your soil with nutrients. When mulch seems to be too dry and brittle, you'll need to remove it and replace it with fresh material. Straw breaks down rather quickly and typically needs to be topped up every year. Wood chips are a bit more durable and can last up to 2 years. If mulch becomes too compacted and starts blocking water flow to the roots, again, you'll need to replace it. If you notice any fungi or any signs of diseases on your plants, you'll need to remove your mulch, bag it up, and dispose of it in the trash. Some pests can use mulch as shelter, and if you notice pests in mulched areas of your garden, you can turn the mulch with a rake or spray it with an organic pesticide. If that doesn't help, you'll need to replace it.

Also, don't forget to maintain your garden paths. If you have them covered with straw, wood chips, compost, or other material, make sure to top them up too because these materials will break down with time, just like mulch on your garden beds does.

Weeding

When weeds grow near your vegetables, they will compete with your vegetables for sunlight, water, and nutrients. You want your vegetables to get all the benefits of sunlight, water, and nutrients so that they grow strong and healthy and taste delicious. You need to pull up weeds weekly to stop them from developing thick and deep roots.

In no-till gardening, mulching is used to control weeds. If mulch areas have thinned, you could top them up, and the mulch will prevent weeds from growing and will also help retain moisture in the soil.

However, you might still get a few weeds here and there. There are a few different ways to remove them, which include hand weeding, shallow hoeing, and using contact weed killers.

Hand weeding is self-explanatory—it means simply pulling the weeds up with your hands. It's an effective method of weed control, but it can take quite a bit of time and effort, especially if you have a larger garden.

Shallow hoeing is hoeing that "fluffs" the soil on the surface. Stirrup hoes (shuffle hoes) are ideal for shallow hoeing. Shallow hoeing works on newly germinated weeds. It kills them and stirs up the weed seed in the top ½ inch (1.2 cm) of the soil. "Fluffing" the soil makes it harder for the next bunch of weed seeds to germinate.

Contact weed killers are organic herbicides that kill weeds on contact. Organic options are non-selective, however, which means they will kill any plant they touch, so you should be careful when applying them. They work best on annual weeds (the ones that complete their lifecycle in a year). They are not as effective against perennial weeds (the ones that die back seasonally but grow back in the spring), but they can weaken them after repeated applications. They typically come in liquid form, either pre-diluted or as concentrates that you need to dilute yourself. You simply need to spray a weed killer on the leaves and stems of weeds for it to work. As mentioned previously, organic contact weed killers are non-selective, and they will kill any plant they touch, so make sure none of it gets on your plants.

You can make an organic herbicide at home using vinegar, salt, and dish soap. To make it, mix 1 gallon (3.8L) of vinegar, 1 cup of salt, and 1 tablespoon of dish soap. The acidity in the vinegar destroys the cells of plants, the salt attacks the tissue, and the soap helps this mixture to stick to the plant. Like all organic herbicides, it is non-selective, which means it will kill all plants, not just weeds. It can also damage lawn grass. So, be careful when spraying it, and make sure it only gets on weeds.

General Garden Maintenance and Care

If you want your plants to thrive throughout the growing season, you will need to schedule in some time to maintain your garden. As mentioned previously, one of the key tasks is watering, and this is essential to the health of your plants. Watering regularly will prevent plants from being stressed, and when plants are stressed, they're more prone to diseases and pests. If you don't water your plants regularly, you won't get a great harvest.

Apart from watering your plants, there are a few things you need to keep on top of, such as pruning your plants, removing dead/straggly plants and composting them, providing support for plants that need it, and preventing animals from eating your plants, all of which will be covered below.

Plant Growth Stages

Perhaps one of the most useful things I've learned about plants over the years is how to observe the stages of plant growth. All plants follow the same basic pattern of growth on their way to maturity, and knowing at which growth stage your plants are can help you know their needs better. Plants go through the following stages during their life cycle:

- Sprout
- Seedling
- Vegetative
- Budding
- Flowering
- Ripening

Plants start their life cycle as seeds. Depending on the type of plant, seeds can take anywhere between a few days to a few weeks to germinate and sprout. Seeds need air, water, and warmth to germinate and grow into seedlings.

As roots develop, sprouts grow into seedlings. They start growing true leaves, which look like baby versions of mature leaves. The main thing that seedlings need to grow is lots of light. If you grow seedlings indoors and they become leggy because they are not getting enough sunlight, you can get grow lights to provide more light to them. This will help them grow stronger and will help prevent legginess. Seedlings also need to be watered regularly because they can't store water for very long, so you'll need to keep the soil moist. They can also benefit from fertilizing. You can fertilize seedlings when they are at least 3 inches (7.5 cm) tall with a mild dose of liquid balanced fertilizer. Fertilizing your garden will be covered in more detail in the next chapter.

When seedlings move into the vegetative stage of their life cycle, plants focus on developing sturdy stems and green, leafy growth. From this point, plants need light, water, air, nutrients, and the right temperature to grow. You'll need to water your plants regularly and fertilize them to provide them with the nutrients they need. Regarding the right temperature, plants are divided into cool-season and warm-season crops. This will be covered in detail in plant profiles in Chapter 9. When plants are in the vegetative stage, they need nitrogen, which provides the nutrients that energize the building of new cells. You can use a balanced fertilizer at all growth stages for most plants with good results. However, you may consider using a fertilizer with a higher first number (nitrogen) during the vegetative stage.

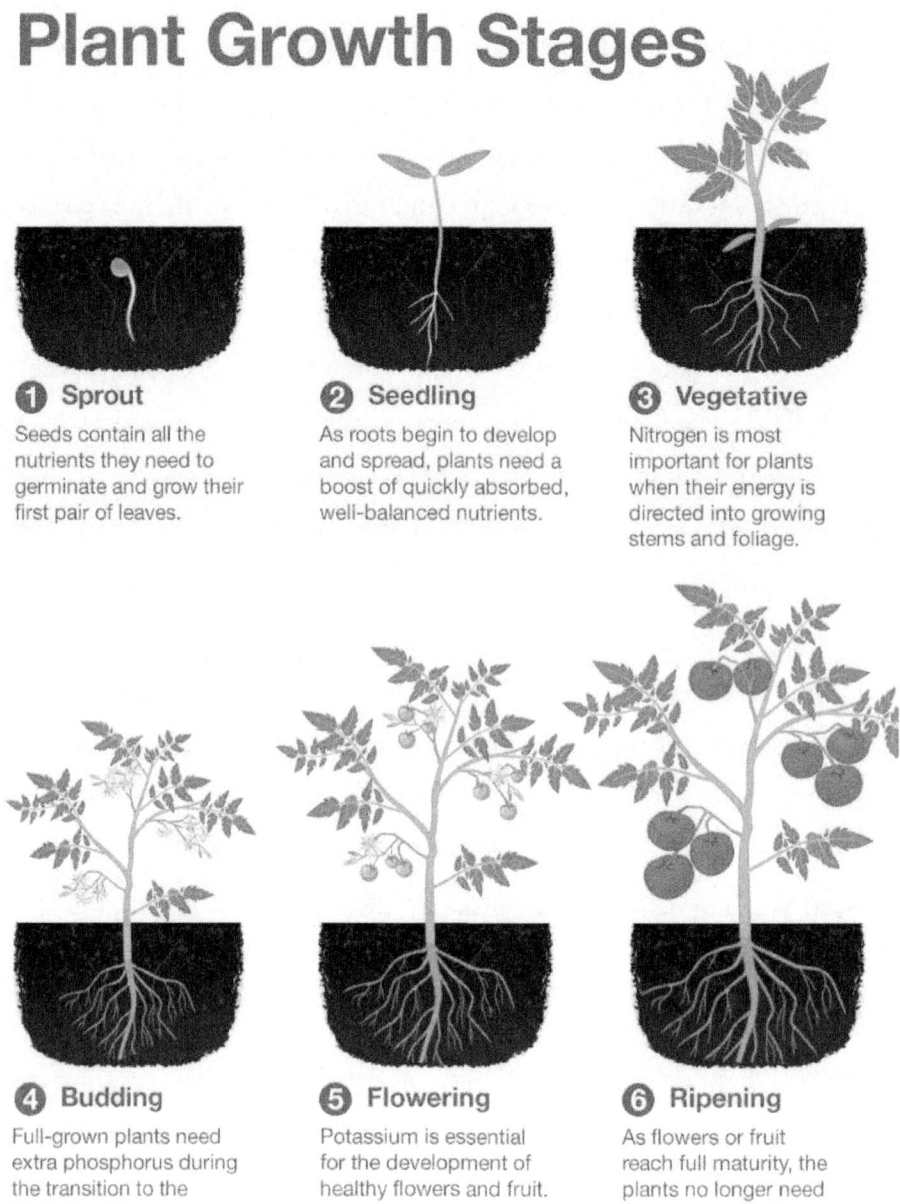

Plant Growth Stages

1 Sprout — Seeds contain all the nutrients they need to germinate and grow their first pair of leaves.

2 Seedling — As roots begin to develop and spread, plants need a boost of quickly absorbed, well-balanced nutrients.

3 Vegetative — Nitrogen is most important for plants when their energy is directed into growing stems and foliage.

4 Budding — Full-grown plants need extra phosphorus during the transition to the blooming stage.

5 Flowering — Potassium is essential for the development of healthy flowers and fruit.

6 Ripening — As flowers or fruit reach full maturity, the plants no longer need nutrients--just water.

As plants grow, they transition from the vegetative stage to the budding stage when they start shifting away from green growth toward producing buds, flowers, and then fruit. In this stage, plants need more phosphorus to help encourage budding. You might consider using a fertilizer with a higher second number (phosphorus) when plants are in the budding stage.

The next stage is flowering, and this is when buds become flowers and fruiting plants begin forming fruit where flowers grew. In this stage, nitrogen becomes less important, and plants need more potassium. Potassium is important for flowering, fruit production, and overall plant health. You may consider using a fertilizer with a higher third number (potassium) when plants are in the flowering stage.

The final stage is ripening, and this is when flowers and fruit ripen and mature. In this stage, plants no longer need added nitrogen for leafy growth because they focus their energy on finishing flowers and fruit. I would recommend that you stop fertilizing your plants in the ripening stage because when flowers and fruit are verging on full maturity, they need a week or two of just water without nutrients so that they can use up all the nutrients they have already absorbed. This process is known as flushing.

Deadheading, Pinching, and Pruning Plants

Deadheading means getting rid of a dead flower head of a plant. When flowers look brown and shriveled or have gone floppy and brown, you can pull these flowers off, or pinch the head off, or some will require you to cut the stem with some secateurs. When you deadhead plants, they will grow fuller and produce more flowers too. They will also continue to bloom for longer because they won't be wasting energy sending it to the dead parts of the plant. Also, when you deadhead a plant, you get rid of dead parts that are taking up space, so more oxygen can circulate around the plant, and more sunlight can get to the leaves when these are removed.

Pinching a plant means removing the end of the plant just above a node on the stem where the leaves are attached. When pinching a plant, you remove the end set of leaves or buds, and in response, the plant sends out two new branches (also known as lateral stems), which results in more leaves and flowers. Pinching encourages branching on plants. It works especially well with herbs because it allows them to produce more desirable stems and leaves. It can also help keep plants compact. By pinching stems, you force the plant to focus on regrowing lost stems rather than growing tall. You can pinch your plants once they have formed a few pairs of leaves on the stem. You don't need to pinch your plants often—most plants can benefit from one or two pinching sessions during the growing season.

Pruning is removing parts of plants, trees, or vines that are not essential to growth or production and are no longer visually pleasing. If you prune any dead, damaged, or diseased bits of plants, this will help them to be healthy. When you're pruning a shrub or a tree, it's advisable to use varying lengths when cutting to make it look more natural, and you should be cutting branches just above buds or where a branch unites with another.

It's worth checking the guidelines for plants because some plants prefer to be pruned in late winter or early spring, whereas others should be pruned after they have bloomed in the spring. When you go to prune your plants, don't prune them in the hottest part of the day. If you're pruning deciduous plants (plants drop their leaves at the end of every growing season), early spring is a good time for this because the cuts will have plenty of time to heal before winter.

If your plants have grown really well but your garden beds or raised beds are overcrowded and the plants don't have room to grow, then pruning the plants can help.

Herbs should be given a regular trim. Some herbs will grow flowers, such as basil and cilantro (coriander). When they grow flowers, this changes the leaves and how the herb tastes. It can make herbs taste bitter, so herbs are typically harvested before they flower. A really good tip is that if you trim your herbs but don't intend to use them immediately and don't want them to go to waste, you could consider either drying them or putting them into ice cubes to use when you need them. Mint can look nice when its flowering, so you could leave a bit of this to give some nice aesthetic appearance to your garden and also attract pollinators, such as bumblebees, moths, and butterflies.

Support

As part of maintenance, you need to ensure that plants that require supports have them. There are trellises for cucumbers, raspberries, and blackberries. You can get bean wigwams, pea sticks, and obelisks for climbing plants and flowers. You can also get supporting hammocks for pumpkins, melons, watermelons, and other heavy vegetables and fruits.

Vegetables need sturdier trellises than vining flowers because they have heavy fruit. You can buy A-frame trellises—they are quite sturdy and durable. Another option is tomato cages, which are good for tomatoes, peppers, and bush squash. They can also be used for pole beans, cucumbers, and grapes. Vining plants will usually climb and wrap themselves around trellises of their own accord.

You can stake tall plants so that the wind doesn't blow them over and snap them. This works well for many vegetables, including tomatoes, eggplants, beans, peas, and more. It's best to place a stake when a plant is still young so that it can climb up the stake.

You can put stakes in at the same time you are planting your plants, and you can stake plants in raised beds too.

You can buy stakes made of bamboo or vinyl-coated metal in most garden centers. Push the stake into the soil beside the plant. Make sure it's not taller than the plant itself. Once you've placed the stake, you'll need to tie your plant to the stake about $\frac{2}{3}$ of the way up the stem, but be careful not to tie it too tight. This can damage your plant as it grows because the tie can cut into the plant's stem. Use stretchy ties to prevent this, such as special plant ties or strips of nylon. You can also use plant clips—they're easier to use than garden ties. Taller plants may need several ties at different points along the stems.

General Welfare

As mentioned previously, you will need to water and fertilize your plants regularly (fertilizing will be covered in detail in the next chapter). You will also want to ensure that all your plants look the best they are able to by pruning and deadheading plants to get rid of dead flowers and dead or overgrown stems or branches. If plants have grown too tall (leggy) and aren't blooming, you'll need to cut them down. You'll have to take out any plants that are dead or not doing well and replace them with new plants. Most importantly, you'll need to check your plants for pests and any signs of diseases regularly. Dealing with pests and diseases will be covered in Chapter 7.

Preventing Animals from Eating Plants

Depending on where you live and what wildlife comes into your garden, you may need to take action to protect your beloved plants. The most obvious choice is putting up a fence, especially if there are large animals, like deer, getting into your garden. Of course, fencing your whole lot is not always feasible or desirable, and motivated critters can find openings in any fence. But putting up a fence is an effective way to stop unwanted critters from getting into your garden.

You can spray your plants with liquids that have an offensive odor or taste, and this is perhaps the least expensive way to repel critters. There are commercial products like Deer-Off (based on eggs, hot peppers, and garlic) or Plantskydd (a blood meal solution) that you can spray directly on plants to make them unpalatable. There are also products that contain predator scents, such as coyote urine, that can be placed strategically around the yard.

You can make a homemade spray that's quite effective in my experience. Mix 1 ounce (30 ml) of hot pepper sauce (the hotter the better), 4 drops of natural dish soap, and 1 cup of aromatic leaves, such as marigolds. Put all the ingredients in a blender, add a cup or two of water, and mix until smooth. Strain the mixture to remove any solids, and put it in a spray bottle. Spray the mixture on your plants once a week, and reapply it after every rain. Make sure to label the bottle, and store it in the fridge.

Critters can often be kept at bay with scare tactics—usually a surprise burst of water or a loud noise works well. You can buy a scarecrow with a motion detector and a sprinkler that sprays water when critters cross its path. Placement is important with such products, so you might need to observe where critters come from. If you have a dog—that's great. Dogs are good at scaring away various critters.

You can also try adding plants that animals don't like—these are usually bitter-tasting or aromatic plants that have a strong fragrance. Marigolds don't need much maintenance, and they can help repel critters. Herbs, such as mint and lavender, can also help keep pests and critters away due to their taste.

Each morning, I go out into my vegetable garden, and I absolutely love tending to it—it's peaceful and calm, and much of the world hasn't woken up yet. There are no phones ringing, no emails pinging, and no chatter. I love the beautiful smells coming from the flowers. I love hearing birds chirping or seeing them come down onto the fence (blackbirds are fearless and happy to be in the garden at the same time as me).

Maintaining my vegetable garden is second nature to me, and it is a part of my daily morning routine and a part of the day that I really look forward to. I make myself a cup of green tea with lemon and head out to take a walk around the garden, noticing new flowers that have bloomed and new vegetables that have started to fruit. I water the vegetables if they require it, and I pull up any weeds as I go. I check the health of the plants and ensure there are no signs of pests or diseases. I check that plants are correctly supported and encourage climbing plants with the trellises I have for them. After I've watered the plants, I take a basket and harvest any vegetables or fruits that are ready. I have them in a plastic basket that I can hose to wash off any debris before taking the produce I've harvested into the house.

Once I have watered and checked the plants, weeded the garden, and harvested vegetables and fruits, I sit at my table in the garden and finish my cup of tea, just relaxing for a few moments before heading in and putting away the harvested produce. Doing this each morning, I feel this is the best way to start my day. It's good for my physical and mental health, and I think it's more of a therapeutic experience rather than a chore. I love my garden and how it develops, and for a relatively small amount of maintenance it requires, I feel I get much more back.

Key takeaways from this chapter:

1. To maintain your garden, water it, remove weeds, mulch your garden beds and raised beds, check plant health, check your plants for any signs of pests or diseases, and ensure that plants that need supports have them.
2. You can use things like outside taps, water butts, a hose reel, or you can hook up a hose to a well to help water your garden.
3. Many variables affect how much water your vegetable garden needs, such as soil, climate, weather, the type of plants you're growing, and more.
4. Stick your finger 1 inch (2.5 cm) deep into the soil to feel the moisture. If it is dry, water it. If it feels moist, wait.
5. Too little or too much water can be damaging for plants. Check for signs if your plants are underwatered or overwatered.
6. It is best to water plants in the morning. Water your plants at the base, and don't splash the leaves.
7. If you have raised beds, drip line irrigation is ideal. You can have it on a timer, which is really convenient.
8. You should mulch your garden beds and raised beds to prevent weeds and keep the moisture in. Keep on top of weeding so that it is quick maintenance and not an onerous chore.
9. Deadhead, pinch, and prune plants so that they bloom for longer. Check pruning guidelines for when to prune plants and don't prune at the hottest part of the day. Prune back herbs—this will help make them taste less bitter after flowering.
10. Support climbing plants with trellises, canes, wigwams, obelisks, poles, and so on. This applies to peas, beans, raspberries, cucumbers, and other plants.
11. Check your plants for any signs or pests or diseases.
12. Deter animals from eating your plants.

The next chapter will look at soil fertility management. It will discuss various techniques you can use to maintain and improve soil fertility so that you can get abundant harvests year after year.

Chapter 6: Soil Fertility Management

Crops grown in healthy, fertile soils result in healthier crops and higher yields than those grown in soils with inadequate or excessive nutrient levels. Soil fertility is vital for plant growth and productivity, and it has to be managed if you want your garden to produce abundant harvests year after year. Soil is one of the most important things in your garden. It is the medium that gives the nutrients and moisture to your plants to help them grow and create delicious produce. A key mantra for no-till gardeners is "feed the soil, not the plant", and no-till gardening is all about replenishing the soil and leaving it in a better condition than before and taking good care of it so that it can take care of your plants and feed you and your family for generations to come.

What Is Soil Fertility?

Simply speaking, soil fertility refers to how rich soil is in nutrients. However, it is also determined by the physical and physiochemical properties of the soil. The physical properties include factors such as soil structure and texture, water holding capacity, drainage, and so on. Physiochemical properties refer to properties such as the pH level of the soil and its nutrient content.

Fertile soil has the following characteristics:

- Has high nutrient levels and contains lots of organic matter
- Has an optimal pH level (6.0 to 7.5), which promotes nutrient availability
- Has good texture, structure, and aeration, making it easy for roots to penetrate
- Drains effectively, preventing waterlogging and fostering root development

While some soil properties can be difficult to alter, proper management practices can improve soil quality. High crop productivity can be achieved through effective management even in poor soils with bad structure. On the contrary, fertile soils can degrade with time if you don't take care of them, which will lead to poor crop growth and yield. Therefore, it is important to manage soil fertility.

How to Manage and Maintain Soil Fertility

The following practices will help you manage and improve soil fertility:

- Balancing nutrient levels using fertilizers (preferably organic)
- Maintaining and building soil organic matter by applying compost and planting cover crops
- Minimizing soil disturbance, which is one of the main principles of no-till gardening
- Keeping the soil covered when not in use by using mulch or cover crops
- Maximizing diversity by using intercropping, planting different cover crops, and practicing crop rotation
- Maintaining living roots in the soil as much as possible throughout the year (by planting cover crops or using succession planting), which will help reduce soil erosion and provide food for organisms like earthworms and microbes that cycle the nutrients your plants need

- Using proper irrigation practices to avoid leaching of essential nutrients and runoff (this was covered in the previous chapter)
- Adjusting soil pH level if it's outside the optimal range (this was covered in Chapter 3)

Now, let's take a closer look at these practices so that you know how to implement them and how they can help you manage and maintain soil fertility.

Fertilizing

Synthetic fertilizers contain chemicals that have salts in them. These salts do not feed earthworms and other microorganisms in the soil. With time, the soil becomes acidic and loses important organisms that are needed to keep it healthy and fertile. The soil structure disintegrates, and the soil can no longer retain water. If the soil doesn't retain water and doesn't have the organisms it needs, your plants won't thrive.

Using organic fertilizers prevents this from happening. Organic fertilizers keep your soil healthy, and they're safe for you, your family, your pets, and the environment, whereas synthetic fertilizers are dangerous and can pollute the environment. Organic fertilizers are slower acting than chemical fertilizers, but organic ones are much better. Some synthetic fertilizers can burn plants because they're so harsh. Organic fertilizers are much gentler and safer. Organic fertilizers will improve your soil quality and increase good fungi and bacteria that the soil needs, whereas chemical fertilizers deplete this over time.

The key thing as a no-till gardener is caring for the health of your soil. The soil needs to contain nutrients to create healthy, tasty plants. You can feed your soil with organic fertilizers. You can also make organic fertilizers at home. It is not expensive and not difficult at all. The most important nutrients plants need to grow are nitrogen (N), phosphorus (P), and potassium (K). Nitrogen is essential for photosynthesis and amino acid production. Phosphorus is required for growth and other functions, including photosynthesis and energy transfer. Potassium is used for root growth and photosynthesis.

When you have a no-till garden, having organic matter and compost will improve your soil and its nutrient content, but you will also need additional organic fertilizers, such as wood ash, rock phosphate, animal byproducts, and manures (especially from animals that do not eat meat). Cow, goat, pig, and chicken droppings make great manure.

You can purchase organic fertilizers from garden centers. Organic fertilizers can be animal based (like bone meal, blood meal, fish meal, or fish emulsion), plant based (like cottonseed, alfalfa, or soybean meal, or seaweed), and there are also mineral fertilizers (like greensand or rock phosphate).

Usually on fertilizers you will see numbers shown on the side to indicate how much of each of the nutrients is in there. You may see numbers like 5-5-5 or 4-3-3. These numbers refer to N-P-K ratio, and they show how much of each of the nutrients (nitrogen, phosphorus, and potassium) the fertilizer contains. Fertilizers that have equal amount of each of the nutrients are called balanced fertilizers, and they may have formulas like 5-5-5. For example, a fertilizer with a formula of 5-5-5 is a balanced fertilizer that has 5% nitrogen, 5% phosphorus, and 5% potassium. Balanced fertilizers work well for most plants, but for plants such as tomatoes and peppers and other fruiting plants, you can use a fertilizer with a higher K number. You can find which fertilizers are best for specific types of plants will be covered in individual plant profiles in Chapter 9.

If you buy an organic fertilizer from a garden center, simply follow the instructions on the label. Typically, you can use organic fertilizers every 2–4 weeks during the growing season on most vegetables.

Types of Fertilizers

There are many different types of fertilizers that you can use:

Dry fertilizers: These are typically added to garden beds or raised beds before planting, but they can also be used during the growing season. You would typically spread dry fertilizers 6 inches (15 cm) away from the base of your plants and water them thoroughly so that the nutrients can soak into the soil.

Liquid fertilizers: These are easily absorbed by the roots of plants, much quicker than dry fertilizers. They are usually used during the growing season to give your plants a boost of nutrients. They are perfect for growing vegetables, and they will help vegetables that grow quickly take up the nutrients they require. Liquid fertilizers are also perfect for fruiting or flowering plants, such as tomatoes, cucumbers, roses, and more.

Growth enhancers: These help your plants absorb nutrients effectively. A good example of this is kelp (a seaweed).

Homemade Organic Fertilizers

While you can purchase organic fertilizers from garden centers, you can also make them at home using a variety of different things. If you have a compost pile, you can make compost tea, which is essentially an organic liquid fertilizer for your plants (making compost will be covered in the next section of this chapter). Here's what you'll need to make compost tea:

- 3 to 4 gallons (11.4–15.2L) non-chlorinated water
- 2 to 6 cups compost
- 5-gallon (19L) bucket
- Shovel
- Strainer

Grab some compost from your compost pile with a shovel, and scoop up between 2 and 6 cups of compost. Add that to your empty bucket.

Next, you'll need some non-chlorinated water because chlorine will kill the good bacteria in your compost. You can use rainwater, or you can use tap water that has sat out for at least a day to allow the chlorine to evaporate. Add about 4 gallons (15.2L) of water to the compost in your bucket. Now you need to mix it all together. Make sure all of the compost gets completely submerged in water, and stir the mixture thoroughly so that the compost and water are combined.

Now you just need to leave the bucket in a place that's not in direct sunlight and let it sit so that the compost tea can brew. Don't leave the bucket in the sun because the heat can encourage the growth of harmful bacteria. Cold weather, rain, and snow can cause the tea to take longer to brew and can also kill beneficial microbes.

The amount of time your tea will take to brew depends on the air temperature outside. If it's above 60°F (15°C), let it sit for 12–36 hours. The lower the temperature, the longer it will take to brew. If the temperature is below 60°F (15°C), you may need to leave it for up to 72 hours. Stir the mixture once or twice a day while it's brewing.

Once the tea has finished brewing, you'll need to strain the compost from the liquid. If your compost tea isn't very dark, you don't need to dilute it. But if it's dark brown or black, you should dilute it with water to a ratio of 1:3 because it may be too strong for your plants. If you think your compost tea is not having the desired effect, you can dilute it less or even use it straight. If it's still too weak, you may need to brew the next batch longer. You can also try adding more compost to the mixture. Compost tea lasts about a week, so you'll need to use it quickly. You can use it every 2–4 weeks during the growing season as a liquid fertilizer.

Coffee grounds are a great source of nitrogen, and you can sprinkle these directly around your plants or make a liquid mix. Simply mix 2 cups of used coffee grounds with 5 gallons (19L) of water, and steep this mixture 3–4 days before using. You can use coffee grounds every 2–4 weeks during the growing season as a liquid fertilizer. Coffee grounds work especially well for nitrogen-loving plants, such as tomatoes, peppers, pole beans, blueberries, roses, and more.

You can also make Epsom salt fertilizer by dissolving 2 tablespoons of Epsom salt per gallon (3.8L) of water. Shake the mixture vigorously, and simply substitute this solution for normal watering once a month. It works because Epsom salt is made up of magnesium and sulfate, both of which are vital plant nutrients. It works especially well for magnesium-loving plants, such as tomatoes, peppers, potatoes, and roses.

Banana peels are very rich in potassium, and you don't even have to compost them. You can simply place these in your soil.

Another amazing organic fertilizer is seaweed. If you live near a beach, you can probably just collect some from there. If you collect fresh seaweed, you can dry it, then grind it, and sprinkle it around your plants.

Some weeds in your garden are full of nutrients, such as chickweed, burdock, and comfrey. You can fill a bucket ⅔ full of grass clippings and weeds and put in 2–3 inches (5–7.5 cm) of water, then let it sit for 3 days, stirring the mixture at least once a day. Keep it covered so that mosquitoes don't settle in it. Then you can spray this over plants, and it will help them grow.

If you keep chickens, goats, cows, or horses on your property, you can use their manure as organic fertilizer. You will need to compost it for best results.

Compost

Compost is decomposed organic matter that can be used as fertilizer to grow plants and to improve soil structure and texture. Three key things that are crucial for compost are nitrogen, carbon, and water. Compost is often called "black gold" because it is so valuable to the health of your soil and your plants. It is also versatile, as it has multiple uses in the garden. You can add compost to your garden when making new garden beds using the no-dig method. You can add it to raised beds when filling them, and you can also use it as mulch.

It is easy enough to make compost yourself from leaves and grass trimmings from your garden, any paper or cardboard from your house, and things like food scraps, vegetables that haven't been used, eggshells, tea bags, coffee grounds, fruit scraps, and so on.

You can purchase a compost bin or build a compost pile. This choice will depend on how much space you have and how much compost you need. If you have a small garden and not a lot of space, you should get a compost bin. Modern composters are streamlined and odor-free, and there are even small bins that you can keep in your kitchen. Or if you have the space, you can get larger outdoor versions, which are essentially a barrel with a crank that makes it easy to keep the contents mixed. If you need a lot of compost and have some free space in your garden, you can build a compost pile with wooden pallets or spare wood where you can store nitrogen items and carbon items separately, and then an area where these are layered together.

To make compost, you need to mix "green" materials (nitrogen), "brown" materials (carbon), and moisture. Green materials include kitchen scraps, like fruit and vegetable peels or waste, eggshells, and coffee grounds, as well as plants and grass trimmings. Brown materials include fallen leaves, tree branches, cardboard, newspapers, hay, straw, and wood shavings. You should have equal parts of green and brown materials. I would suggest alternating layers of green and brown materials. The final ingredient is moisture. Simply spray water on your compost to moisten it, but don't make it soggy. If it's too wet, it won't decompose properly.

There are things that you shouldn't add to compost, and this is because they will rot and smell bad and may attract rodents or larger wildlife. Do not add the following to your compost: meat or fish, dairy, fats and oils, any preserved wood, any diseased plants or invasive weeds (as these could be passed onto your plants via the compost and keep spreading and growing). Don't add charcoal ash to compost because this could kill good bacteria, and definitely don't add dog or cat waste because it could contain harmful bacteria or parasites, and you don't want that in the soil that your plants are growing in.

Compost should heat up in order to decompose at a good rate. You can start your compost pile at any point throughout the year, but it will decompose quicker in the summer than in the winter.

To keep the decomposition rate on track, you'll need to take the temperature of your compost using a compost thermometer deep enough to get about $\frac{2}{3}$ of the way down. You can buy these online or at some garden centers. Make sure to take the temperature in several spots. The ideal temperature is between 130 and 140°F (55–60°C). If it gets up to 160°F (71°C) or more, you need to turn the pile with a pitchfork to aerate it, which will help bring the temperature down. If the temperature gets to 170°F (76°C) or above for more than several hours, this will stop microbes from working and kill the decomposing process. Try to keep the average temperature of your compost around 135°F (57°C).

If the compost starts to smell unpleasant, it could be that you have too much nitrogen (green materials), and you need to balance it with some brown materials. A properly balanced compost pile should not have any unpleasant smells. In fact, it should have a pleasant, earthy smell. If your compost starts to dry out, water it. You should it keep it moist but not soggy. You would typically need to water your compost once or twice a week. You should turn your compost every 2–4 weeks with a pitchfork. Once the compost starts to cool down and look like a black, crumbly material, then it's ready to use in the garden.

You can add compost in layers to create no-till garden beds as mentioned previously. You can also add compost to raised beds when filling them. You can mix up to 30% of compost to the soil in raised beds. When you add compost to your garden beds or raised beds, it can reduce the need for fertilizers. You can also use it as mulch in your garden as well as raised beds (this was covered in detail in the previous chapter). It will help keep your soil and plants' roots cool, retain moisture, and prevent weeds from growing. You can also mulch your garden beds or raised beds to help some plants get through frosty weather. This will help keep the roots warm and will prevent the roots of tender plants from being damaged.

Intercropping and Companion Planting

Intercropping and companion planting and terms that are often used interchangeably, and while they both refer to growing different plants together, it's done for different reasons. Intercropping is done to maximize growing space. Some plants feed from different levels of the soil, so when you plant them together, they won't compete for nutrients, and you can maximize your growing space this way. Companion planting is when you grow plants together for the benefit of one or both of those plants. When some plants are grown together, they can help enhance each other's growth and protect each other from pests and diseases. This is something that you can do with not only vegetables but also herbs and flowers. It is a great thing to do if you want to make the most of your garden space and live in a sustainable way.

Your whole garden is a place of biodiversity, and both intercropping and companion planting can help improve it. There is a wide range of plants, animals, bacteria, and fungi that live in it, which are connected. Plants interact with one another, and they have beneficial relationships. Some plants will attract insects and pollinators that are beneficial for your garden. Others will repel pests and fend off animals that can eat or damage your crops. Legumes will enrich the soil with nitrogen, which will help other plants grow. And tall plants can provide shade and/or support for plants that need it.

Intercropping is typically done in rows where two or more crops are grown together and at least one of the crops is planted in rows. You can either plant the other crop between the rows or plant both plants in alternating rows to keep things more organized.

When intercropping, you should consider the growth rate of plants above and below the ground. Crops that root deeply, such as parsnips, carrots, and tomatoes, can be intercropped with vegetables that have shallow roots, such as broccoli, lettuce, and potatoes. Fast-growing plants, like spinach, can be tucked in around slow maturing plants, like corn. You can also take advantage of the shade provided by tall and broad leaf plants, like corn and sunflowers, and plant lettuce, spinach, or celery underneath.

As for companion planting, most herbs and flowers like marigolds and nasturtiums work well with virtually any plant. Marigolds will help repel pests and attract lots of different beneficial insects (who will eat pests) and pollinators. Nasturtiums are often used as trap crops, which means if you plant them among your vegetables, they will attract pests away from them. Herbs, like basil, rosemary, mint, and others, repel a variety of different pests. However, do not plant fennel near your vegetables because it will stunt their growth. If you want to grow it, it's best to plant it away from other plants.

One of the best companion planting combinations is growing basil and tomatoes together. The smell of basil repels thrips and moths, which lay tomato hornworms. Basil also repels whiteflies from tomatoes and is said to improve the flavor of the tomatoes. So, this companion planting strategy will prevent your tomatoes from being attacked by pests.

Another classic combination is planting corn, pole beans, and squash (any trailing plant from squash family, like pumpkins, zucchini, or melons) together. These three plants have been planted together for centuries. It was done by Native Americans, and this companion planting technique is known as the Three Sisters. This works well because corn is tall and helps provide support for beans as they grow. Beans take nitrogen out of the air and enrich the soil with it, which helps corn and pumpkins grow better. Squash loves the shade provided by corn, and it helps prevent weeds from growing and keep the soil cool, which means you won't have to water the plants as much.

Other combinations that work well include planting carrots, lettuce, and peas together or Brussels sprouts with onions and nasturtiums. Peas and carrots are ideal companions when you plant them in late summer for fall harvest. Both crops thrive in cool, moist conditions, tolerate a light frost, and mature in around 70 to 80 days. Brussels sprouts are great companions for onions and nasturtiums because they grow upright on their own pole, while onions form bulbs underground, and nasturtiums spread and their leaves give excellent cover, which helps keep the soil moist and prevent weeds. Planting carrots and radishes together works well too because radishes grow quickly and can be harvested before carrots start to mature.

However, just like there are companion plants, there are also plants that don't grow well together. There is proper terminology to describe plants that are unfriendly to one another and don't make good companions—"allelopathy"—this means that a plant may impact the growth, survival, or development of another plant. Plants sometimes do this as a survival strategy because they want all the soil space and nutrients.

Fennel, as mentioned previously, is one of such plants, and it should be planted away from your other plants. Another plant that does this is black walnut tree, so it's best not to plant them near your vegetables. It's also a good idea not to plant dill, cilantro (coriander), or any other members of the carrot family near carrots because they will stunt the growth of carrots. Also, don't plant garlic or onions near peas because peas will have stunted growth.

For companion planting to work, plants should be planted within 2–3 rows of each other. Plants that don't grow well together should be planted at least 2–3 rows apart.

If you plant companion plants in the same row and they have different spacing requirements, you can take an average spacing between the plants. If one plant needs 16 inches (40 cm) of space and the other needs

8 inches (20 cm), you can space them 12 inches (30 cm) apart. Remember to consider the height of your plants for proper shading. Try not to completely shade out any of your shorter plants.

While planting vegetables from the same family seems the logical thing to do, it's not always the best decision. Plants from the same family generally require the same growing conditions, but they also attract the same pests.

Cover Cropping

Using cover crops has multiple advantages, including feeding the soil with organic matter, preventing soil erosion, suppressing weeds, and enriching the soil with nutrients. They release sugars and other substances through their roots—a process which is called rhizodeposition.

Keeping your soil as healthy as possible is important, and we've already discussed keeping the disturbance of the soil to a minimum using the no-dig method. Another option to improve your soil fertility is using cover crops.

You would typically plant cover crops over winter when the soil would be empty or between seasonal vegetables after a harvest. You can, of course, add compost or manure to help improve your soil, but you can also add organic matter by simply growing it in the place that you need it. You don't have to move anything. You can scatter the area with seeds and ensure that they are kept moist until they germinate, and then let them grow. By having a crop in place, it reduces the wind being able to erode your topsoil. When the crop is finished, you will need to kill it by cutting it or turning it into the soil, and it will decompose, giving the soil nutrients.

Cover crops are typically used to let your soil rest and rejuvenate over winter, although you can use cover crops in the summer too. Winter cover crops include winter wheat, clovers, and Austrian peas, and summer cover crops include cowpeas, soybeans, and sorghum-sudangrass hybrids.

You can plant cover crops when you don't use your garden to grow vegetables, so you need to figure out how long it will take for your cover crops to mature from the time you plant them to the time you kill them. Before you plant vegetables in the spring, you can cut your cover crops down. They will mulch the soil below and gradually turn into compost, while the roots will decompose in the soil, enriching it with nutrients. I would recommend that you allow 2–4 weeks for cover crops to be broken down by the soil before you sow any edible crops.

Some of the most popular cover crops are buckwheat, cereal rye, and crimson clover. These cover crops feed the organisms found in soil, like fungi and bacteria, and these produce nutrients that your vegetables will thrive on. Earthworms will eat the bacteria and fungi too, and they will help aerate the soil.

You can plant buckwheat in the spring to early summer, at a time when your garden area will be empty for 6–7 weeks. It establishes, blooms, and is ready for incorporation in 35–40 days, and its residue breaks down quickly. As a grain, it reaches maturity in just 70–90 days. Buckwheat helps suppress weeds and attracts beneficial insects and pollinators with its abundant blossoms.

Cereal rye can be planted in early fall, and it will germinate in mid-fall after the soil has lost its warmth. It typically takes 120–150 days to grow to maturity. You can mow down cereal rye in the spring before the plants develop seeds. Cereal rye can help increase organic matter and break up compacted soil.

Crimson clover should be planted in late summer so that the plants can become established before cold weather comes. You can plant it 6–8 weeks before the first frost at the latest. In cold climates, crimson clover can be planted in early spring instead of fall. Crimson clover is a legume, which means it can enrich the soil with nitrogen. Its roots also help prevent soil erosion and improve compacted soil. It typically takes 90 days to grow to maturity. Crimson clover will winter kill, which means that the plants will die back in the cold of winter, so you won't have to cut them down. If crimson clover survives through the winter, you can kill it mechanically (cut it down).

Oilseed radish is another good cover crop. It can be planted early in the spring to provide a quick cover for crops planted in late May or early June. Oilseed radish has a thick, deep root that can help break up compacted soil layers and scavenge nitrate that has leached beyond the rooting zone of other crops.

Mustard is another great cover crop. It can help prevent soil erosion, suppress weeds, and reduce pathogens in the soil. You can plant it in early spring or in the fall. It will reach maturity in 80–95 days depending on the variety. Mustard needs to be chopped or mowed prior to or at flowering and immediately incorporated into the soil while it is still green.

You can plant cover crops in garden beds and raised beds. You can plant your whole garden with cover crops if it's practical and makes economic sense for you, but planting just a small part of your garden is fine too. Remember, no-till methods need to practical and convenient for you. To plant cover crops, you can simply scatter the seeds and water the area well, remembering to keep them moist until they germinate. If you plant cover crops too close to the first frost date, they may not establish well. When they've grown, simply cut them, and let them mulch the soil below and turn into compost. You should kill cover crops shortly after flowering and before they set seed. This allows cover crops to grow to their maximum size and soil health and fertility benefits, but not produce seed. If you allow them to flower, they will go to seed and will become weeds themselves.

Crop Rotation

Crop rotation means planting different crops sequentially on the same plot of land, and it helps improve soil health and fertility, optimize nutrients in the soil as well as combat pests and weeds. By rotating crops, you can also prevent the buildup of large populations of soilborne pathogens. If you kept the same crop in the soil year after year (a monoculture), the pathogens would build up, and you would have a lot of losses to your crop. Growing the same crop year after year in the same soil allows pests and diseases to get really well established there. It would also deplete the soil of the nutrients that type of crop needs. Planting crops year after year would mean that they would grow slowly and be not as healthy, and you'd get less yield from them.

But if you change your crops to something that isn't a host for that soilborne pathogen, the pathogen will die out, and you'll get a better yield come harvest time. Many soil pathogens die out after a few years if there are no suitable hosts, so rotating crops can help eliminate pathogens in the soil.

It's not a good idea to rotate crops that belong to the same family, as they are often affected by the same pathogens. The term "plant family" is used to describe fairly wide groups of plants with similar characteristics. The most commonly grown vegetables belong to the following families:

- Amaryllodaceae (lily or onion family, also called alliums)
- Apiaceae or Umbelliferae (carrot family, also called umbellifers)
- Brassicaceae (brassica or cabbage family, also called brassicas)
- Cucurbitaceae (gourd or squash family, also called cucurbits)
- Fabaceae (legume or pea family, also called legumes)
- Solanaceae (nightshade family or simply nightshades)

Plants in the onion family (alliums) include onions, garlic, leeks, chives, shallots, and other species within the Allium genus. The carrot family includes carrots, celery, chervil, cilantro (coriander), cumin, dill, fennel, lovage, cow parsley, parsley, parsnips, and more. Brassicas include broccoli, Brussels sprouts, cabbage, cauliflower, collards, kale, mustard, radishes, and more. The gourd family includes zucchini, pumpkins as well as summer and winter squash, which most people would class as vegetables. But the family also includes melons, more commonly considered a fruit, as well as cucumbers, which lie somewhere in between. The legume family includes peas and beans, although lentils are also classed within the same group. And finally, the nightshade family includes tomatoes, peppers, eggplants, and potatoes.

For example, broccoli, cabbage, turnips, and mustard are all part of the brassica family, so do not rotate these because it won't help reduce pathogens in the soil. Your vegetables would be more prone to black rot, fusarium wilt, and clubroot.

Some pathogens, such as *Rhizoctoinia solani*, *Sclerotium rolfsii*, and *Pythium* species, attack a lot of different vegetables, so if you suspect you have these pathogens in your soil, it would be best to include small grains in your crop rotation.

If you're growing potatoes and they got potato rot, this will also affect other plants in the nightshade family, such as eggplants, tomatoes, and peppers. If your potatoes were impacted by Colorado potato beetles and you planted potatoes there for another year, the beetles would multiply and lay even more eggs. Whereas if you planted a completely different plant from a different family in there, potato beetles would die off and you'd stop that cycle.

Some pests will stay in the soil for 5 years or more, so rotating crops isn't going to get rid of them. Clubroot spores can stay in the soil for up to 20 years, and white rot (which affects alliums) can survive for up to 40 years. It's good practice to rotate crops, and this can act as a preventative measure for some pests that are poor fliers, like carrot rust flies and flea beetles. It's best if you can pick a site that is downwind from the previous crop location too. If you plant things like carrots after early June, that is after the mating cycle of carrot rust flies, which means there will be a lot of them, but since they are poor fliers, planting downwind can help protect your crop.

Even though crop rotation won't eliminate all pathogens and prevent all diseases, it's still a good method of disease prevention and managing soil fertility. It does take a bit of planning and organizing, but it is well worth it. When you rotate crops, different crops improve the soil and give it nutrients that other plants can use, such as legumes fixing nitrogen in the soil. A full crop rotation cycle lasts 3 to 4 years. Do not plant an area with crops from the same plant family before that cycle is up. You can plan out your crop rotation cycle and keep track of this in a garden journal with a sketch as to your current year and next year's planting. I have created a garden journal that will help you keep all the important information about your garden and plants in one convenient place. If you'd like to find out more about it, please check page 5 of this book.

When we don't use our garden to grow vegetables, we grow cover crops or cover some garden beds with mulch over winter to help prevent soil erosion. We also rotate crops that we grow in our garden. We've been using no-till techniques for over 20 years now, and our garden creates amazing produce year after year with far less work. There is nothing not to love about no-till gardening, and my only regret is that we hadn't started doing it sooner.

Key takeaways from this chapter:

1. Managing soil fertility is vital if you want to get abundant harvests year after year. There are various techniques you can use to manage and improve soil fertility, such as disturbing the soil as little as possible, keeping the soil covered as much as possible, using cover crops, adding compost to the soil, fertilizing your garden using organic fertilizers, keeping living roots in the soil as much as possible, and using proper irrigation techniques to avoid leaching and run off. Remember, you need to feed the soil, not the plant.

2. Organic fertilizers are better than synthetic ones because synthetic fertilizers contain salts, which make the soil acidic and make it deteriorate quickly. Organic fertilizers are slower acting, but they are much better and safer for you, your soil, and your plants. You can make organic fertilizers out of compost, coffee beans, and seaweed. You can also use banana peels as fertilizer.

3. You can make compost out of kitchen scraps, leaves, grass trimmings, paper, cardboard, and so on. Turn your compost periodically to add air, and water it gently to give it some moisture.

4. Adding organic matter, such as compost or manure, to the soil is the most effective way to improve soil fertility as well as rejuvenate hard or compacted soils.

5. Cover crops help prevent soil erosion, suppress weeds, and enrich the soil with nutrients. Good cover crops include buckwheat, cereal rye, crimson clover, oilseed radish, and mustard.

6. Crop rotation helps reduce pests and pathogens in the soil. Rotate crops (put your crops in different parts of the garden each year) and avoid rotating plants from the same family, for example, tomatoes, eggplants, and peppers or cabbage, broccoli, and cauliflower. If you plant crops from different

families every year, pathogens in the soil will die off because they won't have any suitable hosts.

The next chapter will look at pest control and dealing with diseases. It will discuss various organic options to deal with pests rather than using chemical pesticides. The chapter will also look at dealing with diseases and using companion planting for pest control and disease prevention.

Chapter 7: Pest Control and Dealing with Diseases

Once you have established a wonderful vegetable garden, you want to be able to see it grow, develop, and come to fruition, and you deserve to reap the harvest of lovely, fresh vegetables filled with vitamins to help you live a healthy, sustainable lifestyle. So, naturally, the last thing you want is your crop getting eaten and damaged by pests and diseases.

To prevent your vegetables from getting damaged by pests, insects, or animals or them becoming diseased, you need to inspect your plants each week. If you have spaced your plants with plenty of room between them, this will make them less prone to fungal diseases, like powdery mildew.

This chapter will cover how you can spot common garden pests. It will discuss a wide variety of organic pest control options so that you can maintain a sustainable garden. It will give you information on using trap crops to control pests. This chapter will give you information about attracting beneficial insects to your garden to assist with pest and disease control. Also, common garden diseases will be covered as well as disease prevention. This chapter will also cover how companion planting can help prevent diseases and specific companion plants for disease management.

Common Garden Pests

Pests can damage your plants in a variety of ways. Some will target the roots, some may chew up the leaves, some pests feed on other pests, and some will spread diseases through plants in your garden. This section will cover some common types of pests you should look out for, and the next section will cover how you can deal with them using organic options.

Aphids

Aphids are a common garden pest. They are small, 1/16- to 1/8-inch-long (2–4 mm), pear-shaped, soft-bodied insects. They can be a variety of different colors, including green, black, red, yellow, brown, or gray. They attack a lot of different plants, including tomatoes, lettuce, kale, and cabbage, and they especially love fruit trees and flowering plants. They suck the sap out of stems and new leaves.[7]

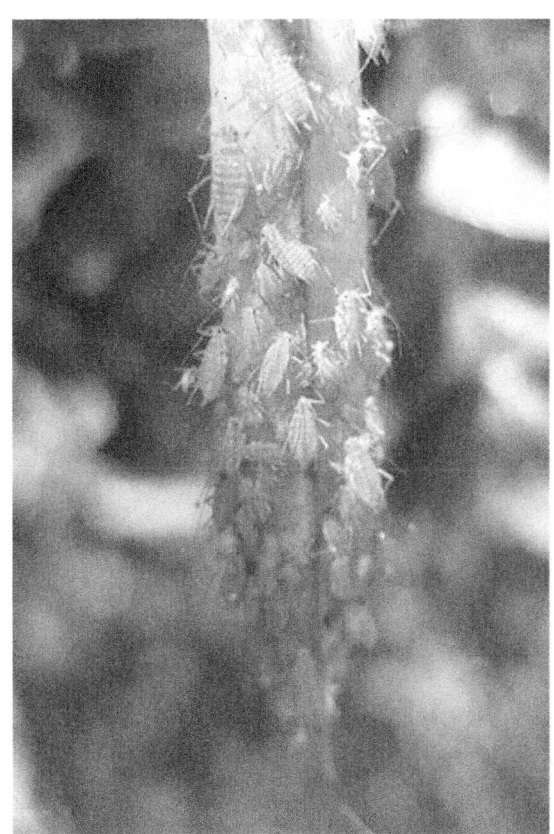

If your plants ever look yellow or brown or if they curl or wilt, do check to ensure there are no aphids on your plants. Because aphids leave behind honeydew (a sugary liquid that is released as they eat your plants),

---

[7] Image from http://www.balconycontainergardening.com/wildlife/633-tips-for-aphid-control

this can cause sooty mold on your plants. If your garden also has ants, this will exacerbate the aphid issue because ants and aphids work hand in hand. Ants will protect aphids because ants like honeydew. A great biological control to deal with aphids is to stop ants first, and this will be discussed in the next section of this chapter that covers dealing with pests.

Ants

Having some ants in the garden is nothing to worry about, but if there are lots of them, they might become a problem. If you have other pests, such as aphids, soft scales, mealybugs, and whiteflies, ants love them because all these pests produce honeydew, which is one of their favorite things to eat. Ants often protect these pests from predators and parasites so that they can continue to produce honeydew. Dealing with ants can help reduce the abundance of honeydew-producing pests.[8]

Birds

Birds are beautiful, and I do love them, but they can act like "pests" in the garden sometimes. They can eat your fruits and vegetables that are ripening up, and they can also pluck seeds out of the soil to eat and dig holes (probably looking for worms) in your garden. They will only eat fruits and vegetables if they don't have any other food, so you can simply leave some feeders with sunflower seeds, which birds love. Many birds also enjoy peanuts, peanut butter, cracked corn, millet, apple pieces, oranges, and even breadcrumbs. Birds will eat some pests, like cabbage worms, so if you want to attract them to your garden, you can also set up a water source, such as a bird bath, in addition to providing them with food.

Cabbage Worms

These are green caterpillars that turn into yellow-white butterflies sometimes with up to 4 black spots on their wings. You will find these on cabbage, kale, cauliflower, broccoli, turnips, radishes, Brussels sprouts, and kohlrabi. They will chew holes in leaves and flowers. Birds eat cabbage worms.[9]

Carrot Rust Flies

Carrot rust flies are small, shiny, and black, and they have an orange head and legs. Their larvae look like tiny maggots. These can affect carrots, parsnips, celeriac, celery, and parsley. They will leave tunnels in your vegetables and scar them.

---

[8] Image from https://www.gardeningknowhow.com/plant-problems/pests/insects/ants-in-flower-pots.htm

[9] Image from https://kellogggarden.com/blog/gardening/how-to-get-rid-of-cabbage-worms/

Pest Control and Dealing with Diseases 73

Caterpillars

Caterpillars can rampage over your garden, munching up leaves, stalks, and stems and making your plants look tatty and damaged. They often show up around late summer and early fall, and they can be a really annoying pest of fall vegetables, like cabbage, kale, collards, broccoli, and cauliflower.[10]

Codling Moths

If you have apple trees, you'll need to look out for codling moths. They chew and bury into apples and leave their larvae inside them. If you see a brown worm in an apple, it is probably a larva of a codling moth.[11]

Colorado Potato Beetles

These beetles are about ⅜ of an inch (1 cm) long, with a bright yellow/orange body and five bold, brown stripes along the length of their bodies. They will eat tomatoes as well as potatoes and other garden crops, like peppers, tomatillos, and eggplants. They will strip the leaves of plants until they look like skeletons. They tend to eat the top of plants first.[12]

Cucumber Beetles

These beetles are yellow, have yellow wings, and they have 3 longitudinal black stripes. They'll go on melons, cucumbers, gourds, squash, and sometimes

---

[10] Image from https://www.nature-and-garden.com/gardening/organic-treatment-caterpillars.html

[11] Image from https://www.growveg.co.uk/pests/uk-and-europe/codling-moth/

[12] Image from https://uwm.edu/field-station/colorado-potato-beetle-redux/

on corn, beans, beets, and other vegetables. They will make holes in leaves and can transmit bacterial wilt.[13]

Cutworms

These turn into brown or gray moths. In the caterpillar stage, they can be yellow, green, brown, or gray. They love to eat young seedlings, especially broccoli, tomatoes, cabbage, and kale.[14]

Flea Beetles

These beetles jump like fleas. They damage young plants by leaving holes in the leaves, and their larvae eat plants' roots, which can destroy a plant completely. They can be found on radishes, potatoes, tomatoes, corn, and eggplants.[15]

Leaf Miners

You can often tell that your plants have leaf miners if you see trails on the leaves. The trails wind round and may look silver or beige. They appear on vegetables, shrubs, bushes, fruit trees, and perennials. These are caused by larvae of a small dark fly. A female fly will make little cuts in the leaf surface and lay her eggs there, and the larvae will tunnel inside the leaf just under the surface. They will feed there, and after 2–3 weeks they'll emerge as adults.

---

[13] Image from https://extension.usu.edu/pests/research/cucumber-beetles

[14] Image from https://gardenerspath.com/how-to/disease-and-pests/control-cutworms/

[15] Image from https://extension.usu.edu/vegetableguide/cucumber-melon-pumpkin-squash/flea-beetles

This mostly just makes the leaves of your plants look unpleasant, but if there's a lot of damage to leaves, then the plant could become weak and even die. One of the most effective ways to get rid of this is to remove infected leaves as soon as you see the trails and dispose of them. Don't add these leaves to compost. Bag them up and dispose of them in the trash.

Mealybugs

Mealybugs look like white, cottony masses that appear on the leaves, stems, and fruit of plants. They have a sucking mouthpart that draws sap out of plants. Plants will turn yellow, curl, and become weak. Mealybugs produce honeydew, which can encourage sooty mold to grow and attract ants. They attack a lot of different plants, including asparagus, beans, beets, cabbage, cucumbers, lettuce, peppers, pumpkins, tomatoes, and more.[16]

Mexican Bean Beetles

These are a common garden pest. These beetles are copper in color and have 16 black spots. Their larvae are yellow with bristly spines. They love all types of beans: green beans, pole beans, snap beans, runner beans, lima beans, and soybeans. They will eat leaves until they look like skeletons.[17]

Pill Bugs

Pill bugs aren't really going to harm your plants, so if you see some near your plants, you shouldn't worry too much about it. However, if you see masses of them, then you may need to do something about it. There are a number of ways to get rid of pill bugs, and one way is to ensure you have food for them that is away from your garden. For example, you could have a compost pile out of the way, and this should keep pill bugs happy and away from your plants.[18]

---

[16] Image from https://wallygrow.com/blogs/feature/how-to-get-rid-of-mealybug-on-houseplants

[17] Image from https://val.vtecostudies.org/projects/lady-beetle-atlas/mexican-bean-beetle/

[18] Image from https://www.thoughtco.com/fascinating-facts-about-pillbugs-4165294

Pill bugs love dark and damp conditions, so they often live under debris in the garden. Cleaning up the debris from leaves, grass clippings, pieces of wood, and so on can help reduce their population. A top tip is that you can put a toilet paper tube around seedlings, and this will stop pill bugs from reaching them.

Root-Knot Nematodes

Nematodes are parasite worms that burrow into roots, and this stops the roots from absorbing the necessary water and nutrients. You can check the roots of your plants by pulling out one plant and looking at the roots to see if there are little balls or knots in the roots. To treat nematodes, once you have harvested the crop, you can bring the roots out into the sun, and direct sunlight will kill nematodes. You can also put French marigold plants near plants with nematodes because French marigold roots release a chemical that is toxic to nematodes.

Slugs and Snails

These will eat plants in your garden, especially low hanging plants in the shade or where it's damp. Slugs and snails can carry lungworm, which can be dangerous to pets. They will attack any young seedlings and a great variety of plants. They will leave holes in leaves. They eat at night and love rainy days. You won't see them often throughout the day.[19]

Spider Mites

Spider mites are very common. They're extremely small, and they have 8 legs and can be red, green, yellow, or brown. They emerge in the spring and eat plants, which makes the plants weak and susceptible to diseases. They attack a lot of different plants, but they're especially attracted to strawberries, tomatoes, melons, and fruit trees. A female spider mite can lay hundreds of eggs and infestations grow really quickly. Definitely look under the leaves of plants because they will hide there.

If the infestation is really bad, remove infested leaves and dispose of them in the trash. Don't add these infested leaves to your compost because the infestation could spread.

Springtails

Springtails love moisture, and they swarm together in clouds that you can see in the air. They can be brown, gray, black, or white. They like wet soil, rotting straw, decaying leaves, and other damp organic matter.

---

[19] Image from https://ucanr.edu/blogs/blogcore/postdetail.cfm?postnum=46093&

They feed on mold, fungi, and algae. They are mostly a nuisance pest and won't damage plants or harm people or pets. They will chew roots in the soil where they're located, which can inhibit plant hardiness, but they rarely do significant damage. If the soil dries out, they will likely find a new home.[20]

Squash Bugs

Squash bugs feed on cucumbers, squash, melons, pumpkins, and zucchini. They suck juice from the leaves and stems of plants. Leaves damaged by squash bugs will be mottled with yellow, and they may go crispy and die.[21]

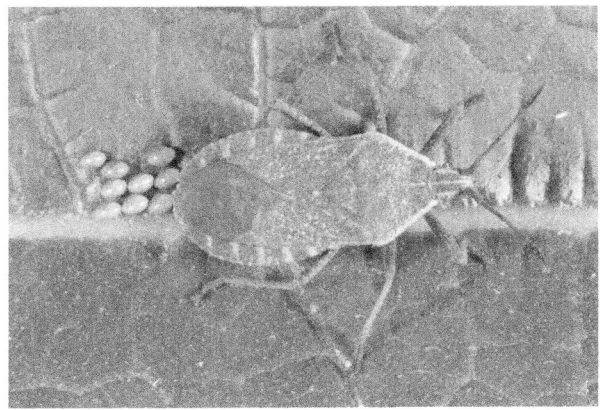

Thrips

Thrips are tiny insects—they are usually 2 millimeters in length. They attack a variety of different vegetables, including onions, beans, carrots, squash, and more. When they're young, they are pale yellow. When they're adults, they are brown or black. If the leaves of your plants are looking dull or have a silver mottling, you may have thrips. If you look really close at the leaves, you may see little black dots on them.[22]

Certain plants tend to get thrips more often, and these include onions, peas, tomatoes, cucumbers, beans, carrots, and many flowers, especially gladioli and roses. Thrips like dry and hot conditions, so if you increase humidity around your plants, this can discourage them. If you get rid of dead leaves and fallen flowers off plants, this can discourage thrips too.

Tomato or Tobacco Hornworms

Hornworm caterpillars turn into brown or gray moths. They will attack tomatoes, potatoes, peppers, eggplants, and tobacco. They eat the leaves, usually the

---

[20] Image from https://www.planetnatural.com/pest-problem-solver/houseplant-pests/springtail-control/

[21] Image from https://www.purdue.edu/hla/sites/yardandgarden/dont-let-sap-sucking-squash-bugs-get-old/

[22] Image from https://www.gardenersworld.com/how-to/solve-problems/thrips/

tops of plants, and leave dark pellets of excrement behind.

Vine Weevils

This beetle will eat the leaves of plants in the summer, and its larvae will attack the roots of plants, which can cause the plants to die. Vine weevils attack a wide variety of plants, but they are especially attracted to flowers, like cyclamen, fuchsias, polyanthus, primulas, and also strawberries.[23]

Whiteflies

Whiteflies are sap-sucking pests, and they target vegetables, such as tomatoes, eggplants, peppers, okra, and brassicas, as well as ornamental plants. They produce honeydew, which can lead to sooty black mold and attract ants. Look for yellow leaves and white ovals under leaves which may be whitefly eggs.[24]

Organic Pest Control Methods

Using organic pesticides is less damaging to the soil and environment rather than using chemical pesticides. Organic methods of pest control do work and can even be more effective than chemical pesticides in some cases. It was mentioned in the introduction to this chapter, but it is super important to regularly check your plants for pest damage because the sooner

---

[23] Image from https://luv2garden.com/identify-and-control-black-vine-weevils/

[24] Image from https://www.naplesgarden.org/container-gardening-bugs-friends-or-foes/

you identify it, the sooner it can be dealt with. A few holes in plants is nothing to worry about, but if damage is getting out of hand, you may need to do something about it.

Organic Pesticides/Sprays

You can purchase organic pesticides from garden centers to help control pests. Make sure to check the packaging carefully to make sure the spray you're purchasing is organic. They will contain *Bacillus*, which is a bacterium. They may have neem oil and copper in them too. You can also make your own organic pesticides from household products or plants. It is advisable to spray both store bought and homemade pesticides on a small part of a plant rather than the whole thing at first just to check it doesn't damage it. Also, don't spray pesticides in really hot sun because this can burn plants.

You can make sprays for pest control at home. Here are some of my favorite recipes:

Neem Oil Spray

Neem oil is typically used when you have a pest infestation, but you can spray your plants with a neem oil solution every 2–3 weeks as a preventative measure. This is good to get rid of soft-bodied insects, such as aphids, fungus gnats, whiteflies, scales, squash bugs, Colorado potato beetles, and mealybugs. Neem oil also works well for treating leaf miners. Pests won't lay eggs after being sprayed, and they will eat less and grow more slowly. Neem oil spray would sadly work on beneficial insects too, so you could spray early in the morning or late in the afternoon, and then cover your plants with a row cover to stop them from being affected. It can also prevent powdery mildew. It does have quite a strong smell. Simply follow the instructions on the label, make a spray, and spray your plants every 3–4 days until pests are gone, and reapply the solution after it rains.

Insecticidal Soap

You can buy insecticidal soap or make homemade insecticidal soap by mixing 1 tablespoon of liquid soap with a quart (0.95L) of water. Just like neem oil, insecticidal soap works well against soft-bodied insects. Simply follow the instructions on the label, make a spray, and use it to spray your plants once or twice a week until pests are gone. Don't forget to reapply it after it rains.

Chili Pepper Spray

This spray is effective against most insects and pests attacking your plants. Mix half a cup of chopped hot peppers, 2 cups of water, and 2 tablespoons of dish soap (with no bleach). Let this sit overnight, strain it, then put it in a spray bottle and spray on plants. Spray your plants every 3–4 days until the infestation is gone. Reapply the spray after it rains.

Garlic Spray

This is great for getting rid of pest and insect infestations. You can make this out of a head of garlic, a tablespoon of dish soap (with no bleach), 2 tablespoons of vegetable oil, and 2 cups of water. Mix the ingredients together, and allow the mixture to sit overnight. Then put it in a spray bottle and spray on plants. Garlic has fungicidal effects, and it's good for getting rid of aphids, squash bugs, whiteflies, and other pests. Spray your plants every 3–4 days until pests are gone. Reapply the spray after it rains.

Oil Spray

This solution is super easy to make. It works great against aphids, mealybugs, mites, leaf miners, whiteflies, and beetle larvae. Simply mix a tablespoon of vegetable oil, 2 tablespoons of baking soda, 1 teaspoon of dish soap, and 2 quarts (1.9 L) of water. Put the mixture into a spray bottle, and spray it on affected plants. Spray as necessary until pests are gone.

Soap Spray

This will help get rid of pests and insects and will keep your plants safe. Soap spray works well against aphids, whiteflies, mealybugs, thrips, spider mites, and other soft-bodied pests and insects. It doesn't work well against larger insects, such as caterpillars, sawflies, and beetle larvae, however. Simply mix 2 teaspoons of dish soap with a quart (0.95 L) of water. The insects become dehydrated and die when you spray them with this. You will need to spray your plants every 4–7 days until pests are gone, and don't forget to reapply the solution after it rains.

Apart from sprays, there are other organic methods to deal with pests:

Water

You can spray your plants with a hose to remove pests like aphids, spider mites, and thrips, but don't blast your plants with water because this can damage them.

Remove Pests by Hand

You can pick off some pests by hand. This is easy to do this with snails, slugs, caterpillars, Colorado potato beetles, and squash bugs. Most insects won't harm you, but you can wear rubber gloves just in case. You will need to kill the insects or place them in a plastic bag or a container with a lid that they can't escape from. Keeping your garden clean also helps prevent pests. While fallen leaves and fruits will decompose and enrich the soil with nutrients, they can also attract pests. You can clear away any dropped or fallen leaves or fruits and add them to your compost pile if they are not diseased.

Nip Off Infected or Infested Parts of Plants

One of the best organic prevention and control methods for pests and diseases is to regularly inspect your plants and physically remove any pests or diseased areas. You can nip off infected or infested leaves or buds or pull up infected crops. You can prune off parts of plants that look like they have a disease or pests.

Diatomaceous Earth (DE)

You can use a shaker to pest-proof plants with this powder. This absorbs the moisture from the bodies of insects and pests. It will work against slugs, aphids, caterpillars, and thrips. It will, however, also kill beneficial insects, so be careful with it. You can put it on the soil around your plants. If you have any leaves that show signs of an infestation, then you can put it underneath the leaves.

Exclusion

You can use exclusion methods to keep pests and diseases away from your plants by covering plants with floating row covers, which are made from lightweight spunbonded fabric. These are effective to keep away aphids, tomato hornworms, cabbage moths and worms, Colorado potato beetles, and squash bugs. If plants don't need pollinating, you can keep the covers on all the time. The fabric is generally sold in 4 or 8-foot rolls, and it comes in lightweight and heavyweight versions (for summer and fall, respectively), which also offers some frost protection.

If you live in an area where there are a lot of deer, tall fencing should keep them out. If you have trouble with rabbits, then having mesh at the bottom of your fence that goes into the ground should keep the rabbits out. If you have raised beds, you can put galvanized wire on the bottom of it, and this will keep out moles and groundhogs. You can put netting and mesh over plants to stop squirrels, birds, and deer from eating your vegetables and fruits before you do.

To protect young seedlings from being attacked by cutworms, you can put a toilet paper tube around them and bury it ½ an inch (1.2 cm) into the ground. This works well to protect cabbage seedlings from cabbage root flies and cabbage maggot flies too.

Another exclusion technique is to put abrasive strips of materials on the soil around plants, which can help repel slugs, snails, and caterpillars. You could create barriers with sawdust, wood ashes, crushed eggshells, seashells, or coffee grounds, and all of these will break down and feed the soil with time too.

You can also set up copper or steel wires around your raised beds and have 2 wires close together connected to a 9V battery to create an electric fence for slugs and snails. While this may prevent any further snails getting in, the ones that are already there will continue to eat your plants. You could put copper around your garden beds too because copper has a chemical reaction with snail and slug slime, which repels them.

Mulch helps protects plants from soil splashing on their leaves, and it will also stop pests from laying eggs on the surface of the soil.

Dealing with Ants

If you spot a lot of ants in your garden, try to find ant trails and follow them to see where they lead you. Ant trails usually lead to ant mounds, where all the ants live alongside their queen ant. You need to kill the queen ant to destroy a colony. You can pour boiling water onto the mound, and it may reach the queen through the tunnels. However, it may sometimes not work because even boiling water cools down quickly on contact with earth, or the queen may be deeper underground, and water might not reach her.

Using borax is a much more effective way of dealing with ants. Mix ½ cup sugar, 1.5 tablespoons of borax, and 1.5 cups of water. Soak some cotton balls in the mixture, and put them in places where you see lots of ants. Sugar will attract the ants, and they will take borax to their home, where they will eat it later. Eating borax will kill the ants.

Attracting Beneficial Insects for Pest Control

It is far better to attract beneficial insects to your garden to sort out pests for you than it is to use pesticides. Chemical pesticides will get rid of beneficial insects as well as bad ones and can put chemicals on vegetables and fruits that you'll consume, as well as impacting the environment—water, air, and wildlife. Even organic pesticides will affect beneficial insects, so it's best to spray them early in the morning or late in the afternoon and then cover the plants with a row cover to stop beneficial insects, such as bees and ladybugs, from being affected. If you create a good environment for beneficial insects, they will come to your garden and eat pests, which is cheaper and safer than using pesticides. Insects are becoming more resistant to chemical pesticides, but beneficial insects can get rid of them by eating them or laying eggs on them, which kills the host.

There are approximately 1 million insects that have been discovered and classified, and less than 1%

of these are pests. So, a far greater number of insects in your garden either won't harm it or are actually beneficial to your garden. Beneficial insects are the ones that eat pests that would otherwise munch upon your delicious vegetables. These are known as predators and can include ladybugs, lacewings, and praying mantises. There are also beneficial parasitic insects. They lay their eggs on pests, and when the eggs hatch, the larvae eat the host. And there are also pollinators who pollinate flowers in the garden, and these include bees, moths, butterflies, and flies.

Ladybugs are good insects to have. They are natural predators to aphids, chinch bugs, asparagus beetle larvae, alfalfa weevils, bean thrips, grape root worms, Colorado potato beetles larvae, spider mites, whiteflies, and mealybugs, among other insects, which means they will eat them. You could grow flowers and herbs, such as cilantro (coriander), dill, fennel, caraway, yarrow, tansy, angelica, scented geraniums, coreopsis, and cosmos, to attract them.

Lacewings are great to have in your garden. In their larval stage, they look like small ½-inch (1.2 cm) alligators, and they will happily eat aphids, caterpillars, mealybugs, leafhoppers, whiteflies, and insect eggs. You can plant cilantro (coriander), dill, yarrow, cosmos, and tansy to attract them. Hover flies are also great to have around. They may look like a small bee, but as they move through the air, they are more fly-like in their appearance. Planting dill, parsley, yarrow, caraway, and lavender will help attract them to your garden.

If you're unsure about which are good insects and which are bad, try to see whether the bugs are eating your garden or defending it by eating other insects. Look to see whether the bugs are chewing holes in your leaves or eating other bugs. You could use a folding 10x power hand lens to help you see the bugs better. If you see bugs in your garden, you can make a description of the bug and then do an Internet search on it or ask in gardening groups on Facebook or gardening forums. You need to find out if it's beneficial or harmful and attract more of the beneficial ones to your garden.

Beneficial nematodes will control soil dwelling pests. The most common ones are *Steinernema carpocapsae* and *Heterorhabditis bacteriophora*. These nematodes search for insects they can use as hosts, and they release bacteria that kill the hosts once inside. If you are suffering from carrot flies, you can release beneficial nematodes into the soil near your carrots, and they will eat the larvae. *Steinernema* is a good nematode to use. You can also use a microbial pest control agent called Bt (*Bacillus thuringiensis*). There are different types of Bt. For example, Btk (*Bacillus thuringiensis kurstaki*) is a subspecies of Bt that targets mosquitoes, fungus gnats, and black fly larvae as well as caterpillars, like cabbage worms, tomato hornworms, cabbage loopers, and gypsy moth. Bt var. san diego (*Bacillus thuringiensis var. san diego*) are used to get rid of Colorado potato beetles. Bt var. san diego has a manufacturing process that includes genetic engineering, however, so it's not approved by the National Organic Program (NOP). Bt and Btk are organic are certified for use in organic agriculture and gardening.

Using Trap Crops to Control Pests

Trap crops are plants that are used to attract pests away from your vegetable crops so that they go on the trap crops (also known as sacrificial plants) and ignore your vegetables. Trap crops are planted as a decoy to lure pests away from vegetables. While pests are feeding on trap crops, your vegetables are safe. You can plant trap crops around the perimeter of the area where your main crops are planted. Because there will be a lot of pests on trap crops, this will attract predatory insects, like ladybugs, lacewings, and parasitic wasps, and these predatory insects will eat them and restore the natural balance in the ecosystem.

Squash bugs and squash vine borers are known to cause trouble to cucurbit crops. If you're growing cucurbits, such as cucumbers, pumpkins, zucchini, squash, and so on, you can plant blue Hubbard squash as a trap crop. If you're growing 100 cucurbit plants, 6–7 blue Hubbard squash plants are enough to control squash bugs.

Radishes make a great trap crop because they grow really quickly and attract things like flea beetles away from brassicas, zucchini, and summer squash, plus they also attract beneficial insects. Nasturtiums can act as a trap crop for flea beetles and aphids, and they are edible too. They're great around cucumbers and squash as well. Marigolds are an excellent plant for interplanting, and they also make a great trap crop. French marigolds will attract slugs, thrips, and nematodes. They also repel a lot of different pests and attract beneficial insects. Mustard plants can also be a good trap crop for brassicas. You can have stinging nettles near your garden (but not actually within a vegetable plot), and they will attract aphids away from your plants, while also attracting beneficial insects, such as ladybugs and lacewings.

You can plant trap crops around the perimeter of your garden or between the rows. If you plant around the perimeter, this is good for insects that don't fly very well, such as thrips. They'll get side-tracked by the perimeter crops and won't go into the middle of larger fields. Planting between the rows is better for pests that can fly well and nematodes.

In a no-till garden, planting between the rows is a better option in most cases because you'll have a mix of plants in there. You can aim to plant 10–20% of trap crops compared to your main crop. You can plant trap crops before your main crops. You need to know what pests may attack your crop, and then you need to plant the appropriate companion plant to act as a trap crop to lure the pests away from your vegetables. Dill and lovage will lure hornworm larvae away from tomatoes. Horseradish and tansy will lure Colorado potato beetles away from potatoes. Marigolds will keep nematodes away from vegetables. Basil and marigolds are good to keep thrips away from garlic. Chervil will keep slugs away from vegetables. Ensure that your trap crops are kept healthy too. If you see that lots of pests have congregated on your trap crops, dispose of infested plants in the trash, and try not to let pests escape.

You need to have trap crops ready for the right time of year when you'll need them. Aphids tend to invade in May or early June, so your trap crops need to be ready then. It is best to combine trap cropping and companion planting to attract beneficial predatory insects, like lacewings and ladybugs, to feed on pests.

Dealing With Diseases

Diseases in plants are usually caused by fungi, bacteria, or viruses. If you have rain showers and warm temperatures, look for fungal and bacterial diseases. In the summer, look for viral diseases. Nematodes love warm weather but can impact the roots of plants all year round.

Because you'll be maintaining your garden on a daily basis, it's generally quite easy to spot if your plants are suffering from any diseases. You should try to tackle these swiftly before they become a big issue and spread.

If you buy plants from a nursery, check that they're healthy. Ensure your plants have enough water, sunlight, and enough space for air to flow around them. You can save plants from some diseases, especially if you catch them early on, but if your plants are beyond saving, you'll have to remove them and dispose of them in a plastic bag in the trash. Never put infected plants in a compost pile.

If you have been working with diseased plants, then ensure you wash your hands, tools, and gardening gloves before handling any other plants to avoid spreading diseases. If you don't live in a tropical area but are growing tropical plants, these may be more prone to diseases because they're not native to the area and haven't built up resistance to local garden pests.

Fungal Diseases

If you see that your plants are wilting, or you have noticed spots on your plants' leaves, or if you can see rotten plant stems, this could be due to a fungal disease. Fungi thrive in dark and damp conditions, so too much rainfall can cause fungal diseases in plants. To prevent fungal diseases from occurring, water your plants at the base, and make sure that plenty of air can circulate around your plants and that all your plants get a good amount of sunlight.

Fungicides are used to treat fungal diseases, although not all diseases can be treated by fungicides. You can purchase organic fungicides, such as neem oil, horticultural oil, copper, sulfur, bicarbonates, and others, from garden centers. If you use copper fungicides for an extended period of time, copper levels can build up in the soil and kill earthworms and other beneficial organisms. Neem oil fungicides affect beneficial insects, so try to use them early in the morning or in the evening. You can also make homemade organic fungicides with baking soda or apple cider vinegar.

To make fungicide with baking soda, mix 4 teaspoons of baking soda and 1 teaspoon of mild soap with a gallon (3.8L) of water. This fungicide recipe works especially well for stopping powdery mildew. Mix all the ingredients together, and put the mixture in a spray bottle. Spray all infected leaves top and bottom, and make sure to cover all the leaves with a thick layer of the mixture so that it drips off the leaves. It can be a good idea to spray the entire plant and not just infected leaves because fungus could be hiding where you can't see it.

To make apple cider vinegar fungicide, mix 4 tablespoons of apple cider vinegar with a gallon (3.8L) of water. This simple recipe has helped me save dozens, if not hundreds, of plants. Try to spray this mixture early in the day so that the sun and acid don't burn your plants. This also works well as a preventative spray. You can spray it every 2–3 weeks just in case.

You can also mix 1 quart (0.95L) of warm water, 1 teaspoon of mouthwash, and 1 tablespoon of hydrogen peroxide to make another good homemade fungicide. Mix all the ingredients together, and spray your plants until the fungus is gone.

Below you will find a list of fungal diseases and their symptoms:

Anthracnose

This fungal disease attacks tree leaves and garden vegetables, including beans, tomatoes, cucumbers, spinach, and watermelons. It is caused by a fungus and cool, wet weather.

If your plants have anthracnose, their leaves will have black, tan, or red spots as well as lesions, and the leaves may become yellow and drop off. This is a fungal disease that tends to happen in late spring and early summer. Remove infected leaves and also collect and destroy any fallen leaves. Thin your plants so that air can circulate around them. You can spray the leaves with a copper or neem oil fungicide too.[25]

Black Spot

Black spot displays itself as black spots on leaves that go yellow and then die. If plants are in the shade and too close together, this can cause this fungal disease. To prevent black spot, ensure your plants have plenty of space so that air can circulate around them. Also, make sure you water your plants at the base, get rid of infected leaves, and spray them with a sulfur, copper, or neem oil fungicide if you notice this. Homemade baking soda fungicide works well against black spot too.[26]

Blight

Blight refers to a specific symptom affecting plants in response to infection by a pathogenic organism. It is caused by fungi, which survive on infected plants or in plant debris. This can impact tomatoes, potatoes, and eggplants. There will be dark spots at the soil level of plants that will climb up toward the leaves of plants. If your plants have blight, act quickly to prevent it from spreading. Remove all affected leaves and burn

---

[25] Image from https://www.gardentech.com/disease/anthracnose

[26] Image from https://www.gardentech.com/disease/black-spot

them, or put them in a plastic bag and dispose of them in the trash. Blight is difficult to treat once it's established, but you can spray your plants with a copper fungicide in early stages of the disease.[27]

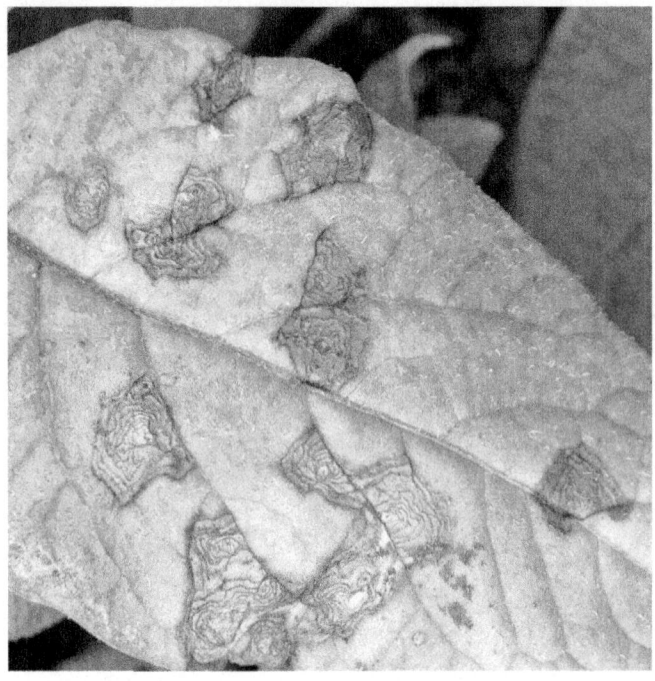

Clubroot

This is a soilborne fungal disease that can attack broccoli, cauliflower, cabbage, Brussels sprouts, radishes, and turnips. Plants don't grow well when they have it, and if you pull them up, they will have bulky roots. Leaves may go yellow and drop. Fungicides will not treat clubroot, and once it's in the soil, it can stay there for 20 years. It only attacks most brassicas, so you can rotate crops to get rid of it. Clubroot prefers acidic soil, so you can amend the pH level of your soil by adding hydrated lime, which will make the soil less acidic (increase its pH level). Determining the amounts of lime you need can be quite complicated, but your local garden center should be able to help you with that.[28]

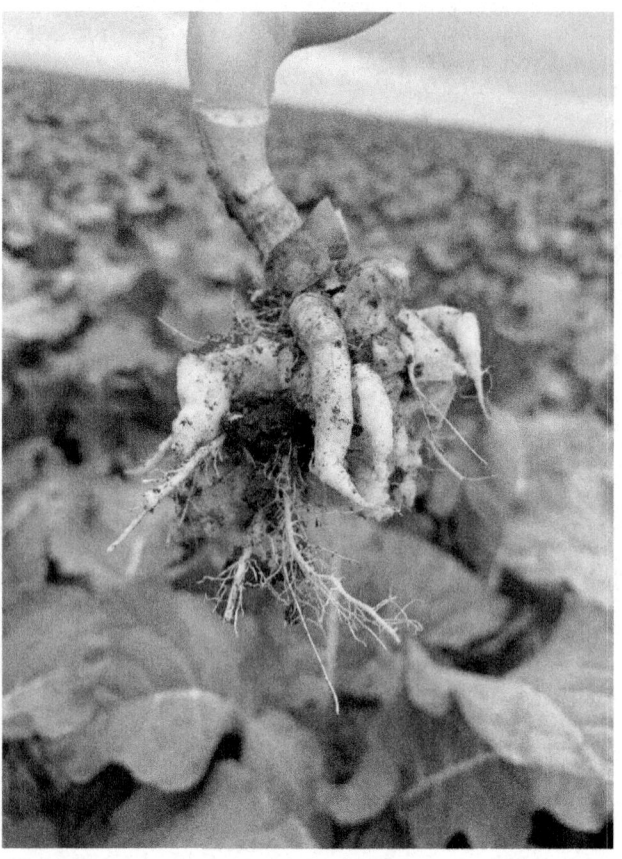

Damping Off

This is a soilborne fungal disease that kills seedlings. Their stems and roots will rot if they have damping off, and healthy-looking seedlings can just keel over and die. It mostly happens when starting seeds indoors. There is no cure for plants that already have damping off. However, you can reduce the chances of it happening it by starting seeds in fresh, soilless seed starting mix. Having proper ventilation also helps avoid damping off. A small fan or simply cracking the lid of your seed starting tray will suffice.

Downy Mildew

Downy mildew is an umbrella term for a large number of plant diseases. It is caused by a fungus-like organism called oomycetes or water molds. By the

---

[27] Image from https://www.planetnatural.com/pest-problem-solver/plant-disease/early-blight/

[28] Image from https://ucanr.edu/blogs/blogcore/postdetail.cfm?postnum=42974

time plants show symptoms, it is already too late, so prevention is key.

This disease likes damp and cold conditions. It spreads through air and water splashing soil onto plants. Different plants can have different symptoms; however, one common symptom is yellow spots on the upper leaf surface between the leaf veins. These spots spread everywhere except the veins and eventually turn brown. Plants cannot photosynthesize on these yellow or brown spots, and when a leaf becomes totally brown, it drops. If a plant loses too many leaves, it will die.[29]

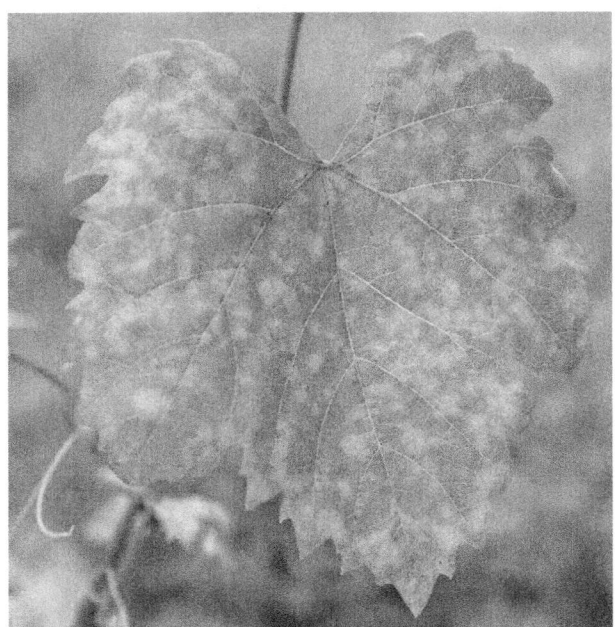

Preventing downy mildew is much easier than controlling it. Water your plants at the base, and make sure they have good air circulation around them. Downy mildew spores overwinter in plant debris. After your crops are done, rake up all leaves and plant debris and dispose of them to help prevent the disease.

If your plants are seriously damaged, remove them and dispose of them in the trash. You can use copper or neem oil fungicides to control downy mildew in early stages. Homemade baking soda fungicide works well against downy mildew too.

Gray Mold

This fungal disease is also known as botrytis blight. If your plants or their fruit appear to be misshapen and have gray fungal spores, this may be due to gray mold. Gray mold causes a dark brown to black blight of flowers, buds, leaves, and stems. Wounded and old plant tissue and flowers are easily infected by gray mold. Gray mold thrives in cool and wet conditions. However, many flowering plants can recover from gray mold when warm, dry conditions return.[30]

The best way to prevent gray mold is to space out plants so that they have good air circulation around them and can dry out after rain or watering. You need to remove infected fruit, flowers, stems, or leaves from the plant and dispose of them, and if need be, thin out the plants so that plenty of air can circulate around them. You can use fungicides to control gray mold.

---

[29] Image from https://www.planetnatural.com/pest-problem-solver/plant-disease/downy-mildew/

[30] Image from https://www.planetnatural.com/pest-problem-solver/plant-disease/gray-mold/

Mycostop is an organic fungicide that works well against gray mold.

Powdery Mildew

Powdery mildew is a fungal disease that affects a wide variety of plants. There are many different species of powdery mildew, and each species attacks different plants. Plants that are commonly affected by powdery mildew include cucurbits (squash, pumpkins, cucumbers, melons), nightshades (tomatoes, eggplants, peppers), legumes (beans, peas), and roses.

Plants infected with powdery mildew look as if they have been dusted with flour. This disease usually starts off as circular, powdery white spots, which can appear on leaves, stems, and sometimes fruit. It usually covers the upper part of leaves.

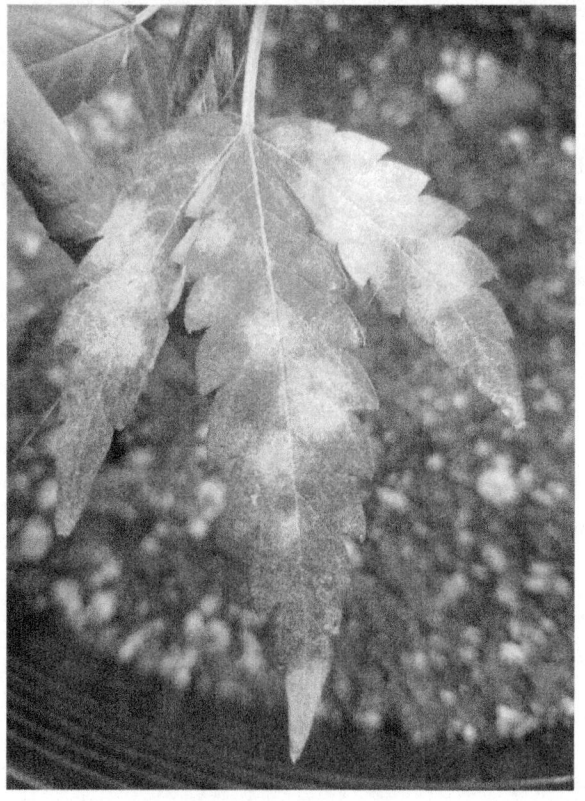

To help prevent powdery mildew, water your plants from the base, and make sure they get enough sunlight and plenty of air can circulate around them. You can protect plants from powdery mildew by making a spray with 1 part milk and 2–3 parts water and spraying it on your plants every 10–14 days. This works especially well on cucumbers, zucchini, and melons.

If your plants have powdery mildew, you should remove all infected leaves, stems, and fruit and dispose of them. There are a few organic fungicides that work well against powdery mildew, including sulfur, lime-sulfur, neem oil, and potassium bicarbonate. Homemade baking soda fungicide works well too.

Rust

Rust is a common fungal disease spread by wind in wet conditions. Spores land on plants and breed. Plants that can be affected by rust include potatoes, sweet potatoes, carrots, onions, beans, peas, corn, eggplants, okra, artichokes, and asparagus. Plants affected by rust disease will have rust-like spots on their leaves. This strips the nutrients out of plants and stunts their growth. It thrives in the summer when it's warm and humid. If your plants have rust, remove all infected parts and dispose of them. Also, clean away all debris in between plants to prevent rust from spreading. There are a lot of organic fungicides that can treat rust, so you can ask your local nursery what they have in stock. Neem oil fungicides work well against rust. Homemade baking soda fungicide works well too.[31]

Verticillium Wilt

Verticillium wilt is a soilborne fungal disease that enters plants through the roots. Plants' leaves will discolor and curl, then wilt, and plants may die when they have this. It can impact tomatoes, peppers, eggplants, cucumbers, pumpkins, and potatoes.[32]

Verticillium wilt can be spread in contaminated soil, so if you suspect your plants might have it, be careful not to spread the soil from around the affected plants on tools or muddy boots. Weed control is important for prevention of this disease because some weeds are hosts, and in some cases, they will not show any visible signs of infection. There is no effective treatment for verticillium wilt. You will have to remove and dispose of infected plants. The best protection against verticillium wilt is growing plants with resistance or immunity to the disease.

Bacterial Diseases

Plants are typically resistant to bacterial diseases. If your plants are healthy, they shouldn't get bacterial diseases. If pests have attacked plants' leaves or stems, then this could allow bacteria to enter and cause rot in the plants, and the plants may look slimy. There are no treatments for most bacterial diseases, so it is best to get rid of infected plants if this occurs and disinfect gardening tools to stop the bacteria from spreading.

Here is a list of bacterial diseases and their symptoms:

Bacterial Leaf Spot

Bacteria can get into the leaves of your plants and cause spots on the leaves, discoloration, and can cause leaves to die. Bacterial leaf spot spreads in warm and wet conditions. Some of the plants commonly affected by this are lettuce, beets, eggplants, and peppers. You can pick off infected leaves, but if a plant has been systemically infected, you'll need to remove it and dispose of it in the trash. There are no treatments for bacterial leaf spot, but you can use copper fungicides to control the disease in early stages. Baking soda and neem oil

---

[31] Image from https://www.planetnatural.com/pest-problem-solver/plant-disease/common-rust/

[32] Image from https://content.ces.ncsu.edu/verticillium-wilt-of-tomato-and-eggplant

fungicides will work too. Remove plant debris, and do not plant new crops where host plants were once growing.[33]

Bacterial Soft Rot

Bacterial soft rots are a group of diseases that cause more crop loss worldwide than any other bacterial disease. Bacterial soft rots affect a wide variety of plants, including lettuce, brassicas, cucurbits, tomatoes, peppers, potatoes, carrots, herbs, and more. Symptoms include wet, slimy, soft rot that affects all parts of vegetable crops, including heads, curds, edible roots, stems, and leaves. There is no treatment for bacterial soft rot. If your plants have this, immediately remove all infected plants or plant parts and dispose of them.[34]

Black Rot

Black rot is a potentially lethal bacterial disease that affects most brassicas. Symptoms include light-brown or yellow V-shaped lesions on leaves, and the leaves become brittle and dry with age. This disease thrives in warm and wet conditions. There are no treatments for black rot, but you can use copper fungicides to control the disease in early stages. You can remove infected leaves, but if a plant has been systemically infected, you'll need to remove the whole plant and dispose of it.[35]

Viral Diseases

Viral diseases are spread by insects, and you may notice yellow leaves that twist, crinkle, and then die. There is no treatment for viral diseases, so the best solution is to pull up infected plants, bag them up, and dispose of them in the trash. Viral diseases are spread by pests, so pest control is key to prevention. Make sure to weed your garden regularly too because some weeds can be hosts for viral diseases.

Below is a list of viral diseases and their symptoms:

Mosaic Virus

Mosaic viruses are a group of viral diseases that are spread by aphids. There are a lot of different varieties of this virus that affect different plants, for example, cucumber mosaic virus, bean common mosaic virus, potato mosaic virus, and others. It can affect brassicas, cucurbits, beans, potatoes, tomatoes, peppers, celery, and other plants. If your plants have this, their leaves

---

[33] Image from https://www.gardening-knowhow.com/plant-problems/disease/bacterial-leaf-spot.htm

[34] Image from https://www.growingproduce.com/vegetables/more-vegetables/take-hard-line-bacterial-soft-rot-pepper/

[35] Image from https://ag.umass.edu/vegetable/fact-sheets/Brassicas-black-rot

may curl, they won't grow well, and you won't get a bountiful harvest.

There is no treatment for mosaic virus, so you'll need to remove and dispose of any infected plants, including the roots, and also any plants near those affected. Since mosaic viruses are spread by aphids, pest control is key to prevention. Weeds can be hosts for mosaic viruses, so make sure to stay on top of weed control. You can also plant virus-resistant plant varieties in your garden.[36]

Tobacco Mosaic Virus

Tobacco mosaic virus is a tobamovirus. Other tobamoviruses include tomato mosaic virus and pepper mild mottle virus. Tobamoviruses are not transmitted by insects. They are highly infectious and very stable in the environment. They can survive on plants, root debris, seeds, tools, and contaminated clothing, which means they can be transmitted by a gardener who has touched an infected plant. It can affect eggplants, tomatoes, bok choy, bitter melon, long melon, Chinese mustard, snake beans, and Chinese cabbage. Symptoms include leaves having a mosaic pattern on them, mottling, leaf distortion, and sometimes leaves may die and fall off infected plants.

If your plants have this, remove and dispose of them. Burn them if you can, or double bag them and dispose of them in the trash. To help prevent this virus, do not smoke and handle plants or allow tobacco products near the garden. If you notice your plants have this, avoid handling other plants, remove and dispose of infected plants as soon as possible, wash your hands, sanitize your tools, wash your clothes, take a shower, and change your clothes before handling other plants.

Tomato Spotted Wilt Virus

This virus is spread by thrips. It can affect peppers, tomatoes, eggplants, lettuce, celery, peas, potatoes, and sweet basil. Plants infected with this will have bronzing of the upper sides of young leaves, which later develop distinct necrotic spots. Other symptoms include ring spots, line patterns, mottling, and chlorotic blotches on leaves. If your plants have this, remove and dispose of them. Make sure to control thrips and weeds to help prevent it from happening in the future.

Other Diseases

Some diseases can be caused by environmental factors, such as drought, freezing, and other stressors. One of the most common diseases of this type is blossom-end rot.

Blossom-End Rot

Blossom-end rot is an environmental problem, which is typically caused by uneven watering or

---

[36] Image from https://www.planetnatural.com/pest-problem-solver/plant-disease/mosaic-virus/

calcium deficiency. This can mean your tomatoes, peppers, eggplants, or cucumbers have rotten bottoms. Blossom end rot will not spread from plant to plant. To prevent blossom end rot, try to keep your soil evenly moist, and add bone meal or oyster shells to your soil to enrich it with calcium.[37]

Disease Prevention

Prevention is better than cure, and that's true with plant health as well. Below are some things you can do to help prevent diseases in your garden:

1. Water plants at the base, and avoid splashing water on leaves or splashing soil on plants. Water plants in the morning to allow any water splashes to dry. This will help prevent fungal diseases.
2. Ensure your plants have sufficient airflow around them and get a good amount of sunlight. If the environment around plants is dark and moist, this is an ideal breeding ground for diseases.
3. Clear any weeds or dead plants because they can house pests and diseases. If you notice any leaves are diseased, remove them and dispose of them in the trash. Do not put them in compost.
4. Wash your hands and tools in between tending to different crops so that you don't spread diseases like the mosaic virus unknowingly.
5. If you think you have experienced damping off with seedlings, then get rid of the soil they were grown in and start again with fresh, soilless seed starting mix.
6. Check any plants you purchase for signs of diseases before you plant them in your garden.
7. Purchase good quality plants and seeds from reputable suppliers that look healthy (and not spindly).
8. You can also purchase disease-resistant varieties of plants. The seed catalog will generally let you know which varieties are disease resistant. Sometimes when you buy disease-resistant plants, they will have abbreviations such as F2 or F3, which means Fusarium resistance. N stands for nematode resistance. AB means resistant to early blight, and LB means resistant to late blight. PB is resistant to powdery mildew, and DM resistant to downy mildew. A means anthracnose resistant. S means scab resistant. BMV is bean mosaic virus resistant.
9. Rotate crops (put your crops in different parts of the garden each year), and avoid rotating plants from the same family, for example, tomatoes, eggplants, and peppers or cabbage, broccoli, and cauliflower.
10. Don't put your plants out too early if it's still cold. They won't grow as well and may be more prone to pests and diseases.

---

[37] Image from https://morningchores.com/blossom-end-rot/

11. Mulch your garden beds and raised beds because this will prevent soil from splashing onto the plants. It will also help retain moisture and reduce weeds.
12. Try to prevent pests from damaging your plants because disease-causing organisms can get inside plants through holes and cuts and infect them.

Companion Planting for Disease Management

As we now know, companion planting is about growing certain plants near each other so that plants are healthier and can produce a better yield. They can support each other physically with shade or actual support to grow up like a trellis, and they can enrich the soil with nutrients. They can help one another in many ways, and one of them is controlling pests and diseases.

Herbs are excellent companion plants because they help repel pests, which can spread diseases and also damage your plants and make them more vulnerable to diseases.

Asparagus and tomatoes make good companions because tomatoes produce solanine, which is toxic to asparagus beetles, and asparagus produces a substance that deters nematodes, which can damage tomato roots.

Planting garlic, onions, borage, and horseradish among your vegetables can help make them more disease resistant. Garlic contains sulfur, which is a naturally occurring fungicide. If you plant chives near apple trees, they will prevent scab, and if you plant them near rose bushes, they will help prevent black spot. If you put onions with strawberries, it will make strawberries more disease resistant. Borage is good for preventing diseases with strawberries and tomatoes. Horseradish makes potatoes more disease resistant and also repels Colorado potato beetles. Putting chamomile next to any plants or shrubs that are ailing may help heal them, as they are naturally anti-fungal.

We had an infestation of ants in our vegetable garden, and we also had aphids. They often go hand in hand because ants like honeydew that is left from aphids sucking the sap out of leaves and stems. Ants can damage things like corn, cucumbers, watermelons, potatoes, and okra. First, we sprayed plants that had aphids on them with a hose to remove them. Then we made a neem oil spray to spray on plants infested by aphids. We knew that once the aphids are gone, the ants would go too. We sprayed the infested plants every 3–4 days for a few weeks, just to be sure we dealt with the infestation, and aphids indeed disappeared. Shortly after, ants were gone too.

Key takeaways from this chapter:
1. Common pests include aphids, caterpillars, carrot rust flies, codling moths, Colorado potato beetles, Mexican bean beetles, slugs, snails, tomato or tobacco hornworms, and whiteflies.
2. You can make organic sprays to repel pests with chili peppers, garlic, neem oil, vegetable oil, and soap.
3. You can nip off leaves and buds that show evidence of pests and/or diseases and dispose of them in the trash. You can also pick off pests by hand.
4. You can cover plants with floating row covers, netting, or mesh and have barriers, such as

sawdust, wood shavings, or eggshells, to keep pests away from your plants.

5. Some insects, such as ladybugs and lacewings, are natural predators to pests and will eat them. You can attract predatory insects by planting flowers and flowering herbs.

6. You can plant trap crops around the perimeter of the area where your crops are planted, or you can plant them between the rows of vegetables. Some examples of traps crops include radishes, horseradish, dill, marigolds, and nasturtiums.

7. Plant diseases can be caused by fungi, bacteria, or viruses.

8. To prevent diseases, water your plants at the base, and avoid getting water on the leaves or splashing them with soil. You can thin your crops out to improve air circulation. If your plants have signs of diseases, you may need to remove and dispose of diseased parts, like leaves, or sometimes whole plants. Check plants from nurseries before buying them. Buy disease-resistant plant seeds. You will find code letters on them that indicate which diseases they are resistant to.

9. You can use companion planting to help repel pests and improve the disease resistance of your plants.

The next chapter will give you information on how you can tell if it's the right time to harvest your vegetables, fruits, and herbs, the signs to look out for, and how to harvest them. It will also cover how you can store your harvest to get the most out of it.

Chapter 8: Time to Harvest the Bounty

So, you've started your no-till garden and took good care of your plants during the growing season. You've ensured that your soil is as healthy as possible, and you've been watering and weeding your garden dutifully. You've done your best to control pests and attract beneficial insects and pollinators to your garden. All of these things should have given your vegetables, fruits, and herbs the optimum conditions to thrive. It's now time for the exciting part of harvesting your bounty!

So, this chapter will cover when you should harvest your crops and how you can tell they're ready to harvest. It will also cover how you should store your harvest to keep it fresh and preserved.

When and How to Harvest Your Vegetables

While seed packets provide information on how long it takes for plants to reach maturity—and this is a helpful guide—there are numerous factors that can change this, including the weather, the quality of your soil, whether your plants got enough water, and so on. But vegetables themselves give some clues as to whether they are mature, and this chapter will help you learn about these.

Some vegetables taste best when they are tender and immature. Things like peas, salad greens, zucchini, cucumbers, beans, potatoes, radishes, cabbage, broccoli, cauliflower, summer squash, and turnips fall into this category. Other plants need to ripen on the vine, such as tomatoes, melons, and winter squash. Most herbs should be harvested before they flower because when they do, they lose their flavor.

It is important to regularly check whether your vegetables are ready to be harvested because if you leave some vegetables for too long, they can become tough or overripe. For example, beans can become tough if left for too long, and zucchini can become overripe.

Before you start harvesting, there are certain tools that will come in handy. These include a clean, food-safe container that you can put your harvest in—this could be a stainless steel bowl, a plastic bowl, or a basket. You will need scissors or pruners and food-safe wipes or soap to be able to clean your tools. Ensure that you have washed your hands and tools before harvesting to avoid spreading any diseases.

For lettuce, kale, and peas, you can pinch off leaves and peas by hand. With lettuce and other leafy vegetables that sprout from the center of the plant, if you're just taking a few leaves and not harvesting the entire thing, then take the outer leaves first so that the plant can continue to grow. If something doesn't come off easily, you can use scissors or a knife. If you have root crops, like potatoes or beets, then you may need to use a fork to harvest them. With herbs and salad leaves, you can use scissors to snip off the leaves, and it's best to take the leaves from around the base of the plant first so that the plant can continue to grow.

Typically, it's best to harvest plants when the temperature is lower—in the morning or later in the evening—because plants will be less stressed. After the morning dew has dried is a good time to harvest. If you were to pick vegetables in midday heat, it can cause leafy vegetables to wilt. Don't harvest vegetables if it's wet because you could easily spread fungal diseases in wet conditions.

You can harvest daily. If you have too much produce, you can store it (this will be covered later in this chapter) or share it with friends, family, and neighbors. Storing your harvest is not the only way to preserve it, of course. You can preserve your harvest with pickling, canning, making jams, freezing, and drying, and I could write a book about it. In fact, I did, and I'd like you to have it for free as a way of saying thanks for purchasing this book. To get your free eBook about 5 easy ways to preserve your harvest, please scan the QR code on page 4 with your phone camera or send me an email to maxbarnesbooks@gmail.com and I will send you the free eBook.

Below you will find information on how to harvest different vegetables:

Arugula: Cut off leaves when they have reached 2–3 inches (5–7.5 cm). Younger leaves taste best. Older leaves can be bitter.

Asparagus: It's ready to harvest when the spears are 6–8 inches (15–20 cm) long and as thick as your pinky finger. Cut the spears with a knife at soil level. Usually, you can harvest asparagus for 4–8 weeks. If you grow asparagus from seed, it can take 3 years before the plant is productive.

Beans: They're ready to harvest when they're as thick as a pencil and you can easily snap a pod in two. You should aim to harvest every day or two.

Beets: They should be dug up when their roots are 1.5–2.5 inches (4–6.5 cm) in diameter. You can also harvest and eat the green tops and have them in salads, steamed, or stir-fried.

Bok choy: When it's 12 inches (30 cm), you can either take the whole plant and cut it with a knife at the roots, or take outer leaves with a knife, or cut all the stems to about an inch (2.5 cm) in height, and new leaves will then start to appear.

Broccoli: When it's 3–6 inches (7.5–15 cm) in diameter, cut the stalk 6 inches (15 cm) below the head. Broccoli grown at home won't get to the sizes that you find in a supermarket.

Brussels sprouts: When the sprouts are 1–1.5 inches (2.5–4 cm) in diameter, start harvesting at the bottom of the stalk where the sprouts are more mature, then move up. You can twist them off or cut them off with a knife.

Cabbage: When the head is a bit bigger than a softball, harvest the cabbage. If you leave it too long, it may split open.

Carrots: Harvest when they're 1 inch (2.5 cm) in diameter.

Cauliflower: It needs to be watched carefully, and you should harvest it before the head separates, or turns yellow, or gets brown spots. Cut with a knife below the head, ensuring you have some leaves attached to stop it from drying out.

Chard: When the leaves are 6 inches (15 cm) long, you can snip them off from the outside of the plant.

Corn: When silks go dry and brown (about 3 weeks after forming) and if the ear (the spiked part of the corn plant that contains kernels) feels rounded, it can be harvested. If it tapers and feels thin at the tip, it's not ready. If you nick a kernel with your finger, it should be succulent and have a milky substance come out. Pick corn in the morning, and place it in the fridge until cooking.

Cucumbers: Harvest them when they're 2–6 inches (5–15 cm) long. The skin should be dark, green, and glossy. If it's dull or yellow, the cucumber is past its best.

Eggplants: Harvest them when their skin is even colored and glossy. If it's dull and the eggplant is soft, it's overripe. Cut eggplants off a plant using a pruner or knife.

Garlic: If you have planted garlic in the spring, it will be ready mid-summer to early fall. If you've planted it in the fall, it will be ready in early summer. You can tell if it's the right time to harvest garlic when the leaves have turned yellow. You should carefully dig up garlic using a fork, being careful not to bruise or damage it. Then garlic needs to be dried in a single layer in the sun, ideally under a cloche, or in a greenhouse or a shed for 2–4 weeks. When the leaves are dry, you can cut off the stalks.

Kale: When the leaves are 6–8 inches (15–20 cm), they're ready to harvest. You can snap them off or use a knife. Harvest the outer leaves at the base of the plant first.

Kohlrabi: When the globes are 2 inches (5 cm) in diameter, they're ready to be harvested. Cut the globe at the root with a knife.

Leeks: Harvest when they're 1 inch (2.5 cm) in diameter. Use a garden fork to loosen the soil, then pull them up from the ground. You can leave leeks in the ground over winter and harvest when needed.

Lettuce: Harvest when it's about 6 inches (15 cm) in diameter. Use a knife to sever the head from the roots. With lettuce leaves, you can harvest them when they are 3–4 inches (7.5–10 cm) long by cutting them off with scissors from the outside. Lettuce tastes best early in the day. If you do pick it later in the day, refresh the leaves in cold water for 30 mins, dry them with paper towels, then place in a plastic bag in the fridge.

Melons: With cantaloupes, they're ready to harvest when the stem pulls easily from the melon and they smell sweet when sniffed. With honeydews, they're ready to harvest when the flower end is softer, and the rind is white or yellow. Cut melons from the vine with a knife.

Mustard greens: Use scissors or a knife to harvest the leaves when they are young, tender, and mild. Harvest leaves from the outside of the plant.

Onions: When they're about 1–2 inches (2.5–5 cm) in diameter and when more than ⅔ of the tops have dried and fallen over, they're ready to be harvested. You should be able to pull them from the ground with your hands in most cases. You can use a fork to help if they're not coming out easily. Hang them up in the sun or somewhere dry for 1–2 weeks. When the necks are dry, trim the roots and store in a cool, dry space.

Parsnips: Harvest after a few frosts for sweeter tasting parsnips. You can also leave them in the ground over winter and harvest them in the spring. Cover them with a thick layer of straw or organic mulch if you leave them over winter. To harvest, use a garden fork to loosen soil, then pull them out. Cut the foliage to ¼ of an inch (6 mm). Store in the fridge or a root cellar.

Peas: You can pull a pod from the vine and do a taste test to see if they're ready. Snip the pods off the vine with scissors or fingers. Harvest daily or every other day. If overripe peas are left on the vine, the vine will not produce anymore.

Peppers: You can harvest them ripe or unripe. Use scissors to cut them off because if you try to twist them off, you will damage the plant. You can pick green peppers, and the plant will continue to produce them. If you let peppers ripen on the vine, the peppers will be sweeter, but you won't get as many. With hot peppers, they're hotter when they're green rather than red. It can be worth wearing gloves when handling them because they can burn your hands. Also, don't rub your eyes when harvesting peppers—wash your hands first.

Potatoes: With new potatoes, they're ready to harvest once they've flowered (usually 6–8 weeks after planting). With other potatoes, leave them in the ground for 2 weeks after the plants have died back. Carefully dig them up so that you don't damage them. They can be stored in a dark and dry place for 2 weeks.

Pumpkins: When a pumpkin has a deep color, the stem has started to dry, and the rind cannot be dented when pressed with a thumbnail, it's ready to be harvested. Use a knife to sever it from the vine. Leave 3 inches (7.5 cm) of the stem attached, and don't carry pumpkins by the stem because you don't want to break it. Let them cure in a well-ventilated place for 10 days.

Radishes: Harvest radishes when they're about 1 inch (2.5 cm) in diameter. If you leave them for too long, they'll be hot, sharp, and pithy. Use a garden fork to loosen soil and pull them up.

Rhubarb: It can be harvested in mid-spring. Pull the stalk upwards and twist sideways. Don't cut the stalks. Harvest until mid-summer, at which point they start to become stringy. Don't eat rhubarb leaves because they are toxic.

Rutabagas: These are ready to harvest when their roots are 4–5 inches (10–12.5 cm) in diameter. Cool weather makes them taste better, so allow them a few frosts. Dig up the roots with a garden fork. Wash off the soil, dry the roots quickly, and store in a root cellar or a fridge.

Shallots: They are ready to harvest when they're 1–1.5 inches (2.5–4 cm) in diameter and the tops have turned brown and flopped over. Store them in a dry place for a week.

Spinach: When the leaves are 3 inches (7.5 cm) long, you can harvest them from the outside of the plant. Tender leaves are more flavorsome and easier to pinch off with fingers. When spinach flowers, stop harvesting it.

Squash: Harvest when small and tender. If the skin toughens, it will be very seedy. Cut squash from the vine with a knife. For winter squash, when the vine shrivels and dries and the rind is hard, it's ready to harvest. Let the squash cure in the sun for 10 days, don't get it wet, and bring it indoors if it looks like it's going to rain.

Sweet potatoes: When the foliage turns yellow, your sweet potatoes are ready to harvest. Lift them from the ground carefully with a garden fork. Cure them in the sun for a day, then place in the shade for 7–10 days.

Tomatoes: They are ready to harvest when fully vine ripened but still firm. You can use scissors to snip them off the plant. If you have unripe tomatoes but you're expecting a frost, then bring them indoors, and wrap the tomatoes in newspaper with space between them for air to circulate.

Turnips: Harvest when the roots are 2–3 inches (5–7.5 cm) in diameter. Harvest before the ground freezes. Turnips have edible foliage too.

Watermelons: Watermelons are ready to harvest when the rind underneath goes from greenish white to a cream or yellow color. Cut watermelons from the vine with a knife, leaving 2 inches (5 cm) of stem attached.

Storing Your Harvest

If you're planning on storing your harvested produce away for later use, you can lightly rinse greens and wrap them in a paper towel to store in the fridge. With other vegetables that you harvest, such as tomatoes, peppers, or onions, don't wash these until you need to use them. This will help prevent them from spoiling.

If you want to store vegetables and fruits to eat later, you can store some for months under the right conditions. You need to select vegetables and fruits that are unblemished and check them regularly to make sure any damaged or diseased vegetables or fruits are removed so that they won't spoil the remainder. If you have one rotten piece of fruit or a rotten vegetable, it can ruin all the rest. You can buy wooden crate storage boxes or use shallow cardboard boxes. If you stack these, ensure that there is space between them for air to circulate.

Different vegetables and fruits need different storage conditions. Temperature and humidity are the most important factors to consider. You've probably seen recommendations like "store in a cool, dry place". But exactly does "cool, dry place" mean? There are three combinations for long-term storage:

- Cool and dry (50–60°F (10–15°C) and 60% relative humidity)
- Cold and dry (32–40°F (0–4°C) and 65% relative humidity)
- Cold and moist (32-40°F (0–4°C) and 95% relative humidity)

The ideal temperature for cold conditions is 32°F (0°C). This temperature is not easy to attain in most homes, however. You can expect shortened shelf life for your vegetables the more storage conditions deviate from the ideal temperature. Shelf life shortens approximately 25% for every 10°F (5.5°C) increase in temperature.

Basements are generally cool and dry. If you decide to store vegetables in your basement, they will need some ventilation. Harvested vegetables still "breathe" and need oxygen to maintain their freshness. Also, make sure to protect your stored produce from rodents.

Refrigerators are generally cold and dry. This works well for long-term storage of garlic and onions, but not much else. If you put vegetables in plastic bags in the fridge, this will create too much humidity, which can lead to the growth of mold and bacteria. You can put vegetables in perforated plastic bags, and this will create cold and moist conditions, but only for a moderate amount of time.

Root cellars are generally cold and moist. If you store vegetables in a cellar, they'll need some ventilation and protection from rodents. You can use materials such as straw, hay, or wood shavings for insulation. If you decide to use insulation, make sure that it's clean.

You can store apples and pears—a good tip is to wrap each of them in newspaper and place these in just one layer in a container. You can store carrots, potatoes, and beets. To do so, ensure that you have removed the leafy tops off carrots and beets. Don't wrap them, and place them in a single layer. You can cover them with a layer of sand to stop them from going rubbery. You can store potatoes in hessian or paper sacks. It's good to harvest potatoes when the weather is dry and then leave them in the sun to dry. Ensure that mud is removed from potatoes to prevent mold. Make sure to store potatoes somewhere dark to stop them from going green.

Most vegetables prefer cold and moist conditions, so a root cellar is the perfect place for long-term storage of most vegetables. Storage conditions for different vegetables and fruits will be covered below.

Cool and dry conditions are suitable for some pumpkins, zucchini, winter squash, and onions.

Cold and moist conditions are suitable for root crops, such as potatoes, carrots, beets, radishes, turnips, and parsnips, as well as asparagus, beans, broccoli, cabbage, cauliflower, corn, spinach, and peas.

Apples and pears can be stored in cold and moist conditions too. Produce that needs cold and moist conditions can be stored in the fridge, but it will last less because refrigerators tend to dry things out.

Some vegetables, such as cucumbers, peppers, tomatoes, and eggplants, require cool and moist storage conditions (55°F or 13°C and 90–95% relative humidity). It's difficult to maintain these conditions in a typical home, so you can expect to keep vegetables that require such storage conditions for only a short period of time.

Berries can't be stored for long. Never rinse berries before storage because it will wash off the thin protective epidermal layer. Place them on a paper towel in a tightly covered container, and store them in the fridge for 2–3 days.

If you want to store onions or shallots, these need to be dried, plaited, and stored in a dry place. You can cut the tops off and hang them in tights or netting.

Any leafy vegetables don't store well, and you should ideally eat these within a few days of harvesting them.

Below you will find a table with storage conditions for a variety of different vegetables and fruits as well as their approximate storage life:

Produce	Temperature	Relative humidity (percent)	Approximate storage life
Fruits			
Apples	30–40°F (–1 to +4°C)	90–95	1–12 months
Apricots	31–32°F (–0.5 to 0°C)	90–95	1–3 weeks
Berries			
— Blackberries	31–32°F (–0.5 to 0°C)	90–95	2–3 days
— Elderberries	31–32°F (–0.5 to 0°C)	90–95	1–2 weeks

Produce	Temperature	Relative humidity (percent)	Approximate storage life
— Gooseberries	31–32°F (–0.5 to 0°C)	90–95	3–4 weeks
— Raspberries	31–32°F (–0.5 to 0°C)	90–95	2–3 days
— Strawberries	32°F (0°C)	90–95	3–7 days
— Cherries, sour	32°F (0°C)	90–95	3–7 days
— Cherries, sweet	30–31°F (–1 to –0.5°C)	90–95	2–3 weeks
Nectarines	31–32°F (–0.5 to 0°C)	90–95	2–4 weeks
Peaches	31–32°F (–0.5 to 0°C)	90–95	2–4 weeks
Pears	29–31°F (–1.5 to –0.5°C)	90–95	2–7 months
Plums and prunes	31–32°F (–0.5 to 0°C)	90–95	2–5 weeks
Vegetables			
Asparagus	32–35°F (0–1.5°C)	95–100	2–3 weeks
Beans, green or snap	40–45°F (4–7°C)	95	7–10 days
Beets, topped	32°F (0°C)	98–100	4–6 months
Broccoli	32°F (0°C)	95–100	10–14 days
Brussels sprouts	32°F (0°C)	95–100	3–5 weeks
Cabbage, early	32°F (0°C)	98–100	3–6 weeks
Cabbage, late	32°F (0°C)	98–100	5–6 months
Carrots	32°F (0°C)	98–100	7–9 months
Cauliflower	32°F (0°C)	95–98	3–4 weeks
Celeriac	32°F (0°C)	97–99	6–8 months
Celery	32°F (0°C)	98–100	2–3 months
Chard	32°F (0°C)	95–100	10–14 days
Corn, sweet	32°F (0°C)	95–98	5–8 days
Cucumbers	50–55°F (10–13°C)	95	10–14 days
Eggplant	46–54°F (8–12°C)	90–95	1 week
Garlic	32°F (0°C)	65–70	6–7 months
Horseradish	30–32°F (–1 to 0°C)	98–100	10–12 months
Kale	32°F (0°C)	95–100	2–3 weeks
Leeks	32°F (0°C)	95–100	2–3 months
Lettuce	32°F (0°C)	98–100	2–3 weeks
Onions, green	32°F (0°C)	95–100	3–4 weeks

Produce	Temperature	Relative humidity (percent)	Approximate storage life
Onions, dry	32°F (0°C)	65–70	1–8 months
Onion sets	32°F (0°C)	65–70	6–8 months
Parsley	32°F (0°C)	95–100	2–2.5 months
Parsnips	32°F (0°C)	98–100	4–6 months
Peas, green	32°F (0°C)	95–98	1–2 weeks
Peppers, chili (dry)	32–50°F (0–10°C)	60–70	6 months
Peppers, sweet	45–55°F (7–13°C)	90–95	2–3 weeks
Potatoes, early crop	40°F (4°C)	90–95	4–5 months
Potatoes, late crop	38–40°F (3–4°C)	90–95	5–10 months
Pumpkins	50–55°F (10–13°C)	50–70	2–3 months
Radishes, spring	32°F (0°C)	95–100	3–4 weeks
Radishes, winter	32°F (0°C)	95–100	2–4 months
Rhubarb	32°F (0°C)	95–100	2–4 weeks
Rutabagas	32°F (0°C)	98–100	4–6 months
Spinach	32°F (0°C)	95–100	10–14 days
Squashes, summer	41–50°F (5–10°C)	95	1–2 weeks
Squashes, winter	50°F (10°C)	50–70	1–6 months
Sweet potatoes	55–60°F (13–16°C)	85–90	4–7 months
Tomatoes mature, green	55–70°F (13–21°C)	90–95	1–3 weeks
Tomatoes firm, ripe	55–70°F (13–21°C)	90–95	4–7 days
Turnips	32°F (0°C)	95	4–5 months

I think there is no better thing than eating vegetables and fruits you have grown yourself in the garden. It is wonderful going out into the garden with a basket and picking fresh, organic vegetables that you've grown yourself, gently rinsing them, and then cooking them for an evening meal. I still remember when we harvested produce from our garden for the first time and I roasted the vegetables and made a vegetable lasagna with rich, tangy tomato sauce between the layers and had it with a side salad. To this day, it may be one of the best meals I've ever had. The taste was phenomenal, and I felt so much pride in knowing that I've grown these tasty vegetables from seed and have nurtured them into something that fed me and my family very well. We had so much lovely produce! We shared it with family and friends and made things like pickles and chutneys. I adore gardening and getting all the lovely rewards from it, and no-till gardening has most definitely made my garden a prettier and more exciting place, and we definitely get more and better-quality produce from our plants.

Key takeaways from this chapter:

1. Some vegetables taste best when they are tender and immature, such as salad greens, zucchini, cucumbers, potatoes, radishes, cabbage, broccoli, cauliflower, spinach, turnips, oregano, and basil.
2. With salad or leafy greens, take leaves from the outer side of the plant so that the plant can continue to grow.
3. Harvest vegetables in the morning, ideally after the morning dew has dried.
4. Never harvest when it's wet because you could spread fungal diseases.
5. You can harvest daily.
6. Things like broccoli and cauliflower that you grow in your garden won't be as large as the ones you might find in a supermarket, but they'll be tastier.
7. When harvesting sprouts, start at the bottom of the stalk.
8. Garlic and onions need to be cured in the sun for 2 weeks.
9. You can leave parsnips and some other root vegetables in the ground over winter and dig them up when required.
10. Individually wrap apples in newspaper and store them in a root cellar.
11. Pick and cook corn when required.
12. With herbs, wrap them in a paper towel and place in a plastic bag in the fridge to reduce wilting.
13. Don't refrigerate tomatoes.

The next chapter will look at plant profiles of different vegetables and fruits. This will help you when selecting the best type of plants to grow in your garden. This chapter will give you information on how to start different plants, how much light they require, what conditions they prefer, how much water and fertilization they need, and when they should be harvested. This will help you make better choices before selecting plants to grow. It will cover a variety of vegetables, fruits, herbs, and flowers.

Chapter 9: Plant Profiles

This chapter is here to help you make informed decisions about what plants you could grow in your garden. You will know what type of soil and what growing conditions different plants prefer, how to start them, their sun requirements, how much water they need, how often they need to be fertilized, whether they need any special care, like support or pruning, and other important information regarding growing different types of plants.

All plants can be classified as annuals, biennials, or perennials—these terms are related to the life cycle of plants. Annuals complete their entire life cycle in just one year. They go from seed to plant to flower and to seed again during that one year. Only the seed survives to start the next generation, and the rest of the plant dies. Biennials take up to two years to complete their life cycle. They produce vegetation in the first year, and in the second year, they produce flowers and seeds that go on to produce the next generation. Many vegetables are biennials but are often grown as annuals. Perennials live more than two years—from three years to hundreds of years. The above-ground portion of perennial plants may die in the winter and come back from the roots the following year. Some plants may retain foliage throughout the winter. Trees and shrubs are perennials.

This chapter covers 22 vegetables, 8 fruits, 8 herbs, and 2 flowers. Clearly, this chapter won't cover every type of plant you may wish to grow in your garden, but for a beginner just starting out, it will give you some good pointers as to some of the more common plants you can grow in your garden and what to expect from them.

Vegetables

Beets (Beetroot)

Beets prefer well-drained soils with pH levels between 6.0 and 7.0.

Beets are biennial plants grown as annuals. They don't like to be transplanted, so you'll need to direct sow them 1–2 weeks before the last frost. Plant the seeds ½ inch (1.2 cm) deep. Beets need 3–4 inches (7.5–10 cm) of space between plants for smaller varieties and 6 inches (15 cm) for larger ones. Rows should be spaced 12–18 inches (30–45 cm) apart.

Beets can be grown in full or partial sun, and they will need at least 6 hours of sunlight per day. They are a cool-season crop, and they prefer temperatures around 50–85°F (10–30°C). Beets need 1 inch (2.5 cm) of water per week. It's a good idea to use either time-based (slow-release) fertilizer or compost to enrich the soil when they sprout and then fertilize them again with a liquid fertilizer about 5 weeks after that when they break the soil surface. Beets are a root vegetable, so they need a fertilizer that is low in nitrogen but high in phosphorus and potassium.

Beets typically take 6–9 weeks to get ready for harvest after germination. You can also harvest beet greens to use in salads—their tender leaves taste delicious. You can start harvesting greens when leaves are a few inches long by cutting the outer leaves only and leaving the small inner foliage to grow, which you can harvest later.

Broccoli

Broccoli grows best in well-drained soils with a pH between 6.0 and 6.8.

Broccoli is a biennial plant grown as an annual. You can start broccoli from seed 7–9 weeks before the last frost. Sow the seeds ½ inch (0.6 cm) deep in individual pots filled with seed starting mix. Give them plenty of light and water them regularly. They will germinate in 1–2 weeks. You can transplant them outside around 2 weeks before the last frost once they are 3–7 inches (7.5–18 cm) tall and have 2–4 true leaves. You can also direct sow broccoli 2–3 weeks before the last frost. Broccoli needs 18 inches (45 cm) of space between plants and 18–24 inches (45–60 cm) of space between rows.

Broccoli needs full sun and at least 6 hours of sunlight per day. It's a cool-season crop, and it grows best in temperatures between 65 and 75°F (18–24°C). It needs 1–2 inches (2.5–5 cm) of water per week. Fertilize broccoli 3 weeks after transplanting seedlings into the garden and then every 2–3 weeks after that. You can use a low-nitrogen fertilizer, but balanced fertilizers work well too. You may need to prune them if you notice vigorous growth. You'll need to pinch out newly developing side shoots, and you can also cut away wilting leaves from sides. But don't go too hard on it—avoid excessive pruning.

Broccoli will be ready to harvest in 60–90 days after seeding. Look out for light green buds, and cut them with 4–5 inches (10–12.5 cm) of stem, but leave the outer leaves intact because they are going to encourage new growth.

Cabbage

Cabbage prefers well-drained soil with a pH level between 6 and 7.

Cabbage is a biennial plant grown as an annual. Cabbage can be direct sown or started indoors early for fall and spring crops or purchased as transplants for a fall crop. You can start cabbage indoors 6–8 weeks before transplanting. You can transplant your cabbage seedlings 1–2 weeks before the last frost after they've been hardened off outside for a week for spring harvest, or you can sow cabbage seeds directly 6–8 weeks before the first frost in the fall for fall harvest. Plant the seeds ¼ to ½ inch (0.6–1.2 cm) deep. Some cabbage varieties can require up to 24 inches (60 cm) of spacing between plants; however, most compact varieties need 1 foot (30 cm) of space, and most larger varieties need 18 inches (45 cm) of space between plants and 12–24 inches (30–60 cm) of space between rows. You can check the seed packet for spacing requirements for the specific variety you're growing.

Cabbage needs full sun with 6–8 hours of sunlight per day. Cabbage is a cool-season crop, and it grows best in temperatures between 60 and 65°F (15–18°C) and no higher than 75°F (24°C). Cabbage needs 1–2 inches (2.5–5 cm) of water per week. You can fertilize cabbage with a balanced liquid fertilizer every 2–3 weeks. Compost tea works great for cabbage.

Cabbage generally takes around 70–80 days to reach maturity; however, some varieties can take up to 4–6 months to grow, depending on the type. Harvest them once they have reached the size you want and formed a firm head. To harvest, cut each cabbage head at the base with a sharp knife, remove any yellow leaves, but keep loose green leaves because they provide protection in storage, and immediately bring the head indoors, or place it in shade.

Carrots

Carrots prefer soil with pH levels between 6.0 and 7.0.

Carrots are biennial plants grown as annuals. They don't like to be transplanted, so it's best to direct sow them. You can sow the seeds just after the last frost. Carrot seeds should be placed ¼ to ½ inch (0.6–1.2 cm) below the surface of the soil. Carrots need 2–3 inches (5–7.5 cm) of space between them and 1 foot (30 cm) of space between rows.

Carrots like full sun. They need at least 6 hours of sunlight per day. Carrots are a cool-season crop, and the ideal temperature for them is 60–72°F (15–22°C). If you live in a warm area, you can grow them in the fall and maybe even in the winter. Carrots need 1 inch (2.5 cm) of water per week when young, but as the roots mature, you can increase the water to 2 inches (5 cm) per week. You can fertilize carrots 5–6 weeks after sowing with a liquid fertilizer that is low in nitrogen and high in phosphorus and potassium. Keep the soil moist because if the soil dries out, the roots may crack, and you will get a poor harvest.

You can usually harvest carrots 60–75 days after sowing. Pull one up and see how it is when you think the time is right.

Cauliflower

Cauliflower grows best in well-drained soils with pH levels between 6.0 and 7.0.

Cauliflower is a biennial plant grown as an annual. It is best started indoors. You can start cauliflower seeds indoors about a month before the last frost. Sow the seeds in seed starting mix ½ inch (1.2 cm) deep. Once the seedlings have germinated and plants have 3 or 4 leaves, you can transplant them outside. This should be done about 2 weeks before the last frost.

Cauliflower grows best in full sun, and it needs 6–8 hours of sunlight per day. It's a cool-season crop, and it does best in moderate temperatures (60–75°F or 15–24°C). Cauliflower needs 1–2 inches (2.5–5 cm) of water per week. It needs to be fertilized a lot. You can add compost or well-rotted manure to the soil when you plant them. You'll need to add compost in mid-season as well. Alternatively, you can use a balanced liquid fertilizer once a month or according to the product's instructions.

Cauliflower is typically ready to harvest 3–4 months after planting. It's ready to be harvested when the head is fully developed. It should be 6–12 inches (15–30 cm) in diameter and still compact.

Celery

Celery prefers well-drained soils with pH levels between 5.8 and 6.8.

Celery is a biennial plant grown as an annual. It has a long growing season, so it's best to start it from seed indoors and transplant it outside when it's ready. You can sow the seeds 10–12 weeks before the last frost. It's a good idea to soak celery seeds in water overnight before sowing. When the seedlings are 2 inches (5 cm) tall, transplant them into individual pots. Introduce them to the outdoors gradually because they don't like cold weather. Seedlings should be transplanted outside 8 to 10 inches (20–25 cm) apart with 12–24 inches (30–60 cm) of space between rows.

Celery grows best in full sun, but it can grow in partial sun too. It needs 5–7 hours of sunlight per day.

Celery is a cool-season crop that prefers temperatures between 60 and 70°F (15–21°C). Celery needs 1–2 inches (2.5–5 cm) of water per week. You can add compost at the time of planting, and then you can fertilize it with a potassium-rich liquid fertilizer every month.

When celery starts to grow, you can tie the stalks together to keep them together and stop them from sprawling. You can harvest whole plants or just a stalk or two as you need them to keep the plants growing longer. The darker the stalks are, the more nutrients they contain, but darker green stalks are tougher. You can store celery in the fridge in a plastic bag for a few weeks.

When celery is ready to harvest, the stalks will typically be around 12–18 inches (30–45 cm). It usually takes 130–140 days to grow before harvesting. Harvest stalks from the outside in. You can harvest the plants whole, but cutting individual stalks will keep plants producing for a longer period of time.

Collard Greens

Collard greens prefer well-drained soil with a pH level between 6.0 and 7.5.

Collard greens are a biennial crop grown as an annual. I would suggest direct sowing them after the last frost for spring harvest or 3 months before the first frost for fall harvest; however, you can start them indoors 4–6 weeks before the last frost and transplant them outside when the seedlings are 4–6 inches (10–15 cm tall) and daytime temperatures reach 50°F (10°C). Plant the seeds ¼ to ½ inch (0.6–1.2 cm) deep. Collard greens need 12–18 inches (30–45 cm) of space between plants and 18–36 (45–90 cm) inches of space between rows.

Collard greens prefer growing in full sun, but they will tolerate some shade as long as they get at least 5 hours of sunlight per day. They are a cool-season crop, and they prefer temperatures between 55 and 75°F (13–24°C). They are quite thirsty and need 2 inches (5 cm) of water per week. Collard greens don't need a lot of fertilizing—you can fertilize them every 4–6 weeks with a high-nitrogen liquid fertilizer, although a balanced fertilizer would work fine too.

Collard greens usually take 80 days to grow from seed to harvest. You can harvest the leaves as needed or harvest whole plants. Collard leaves are ready for harvest as soon as they reach usable size. You can pick a couple of outer leaves at a time—use scissors or a sharp kitchen knife to cut the leaves about an inch (2.5 cm) from where they jut out of the soil. They will be most tasty when picked young—less than 10 inches (25 cm) long and dark green. If you want to harvest the whole plant, you can cut it off above the crown if there's still some time for it to produce a few more leaves before the growing season ends. Or if the growing season is ending soon, you can pull the whole plant up and cut the roots off once it's out of the ground.

Corn

Corn grows best in well-drained soils with pH levels between 6.0 and 6.8.

Corn is an annual plant. It does not transplant well, so it's best to direct sow it 2–3 weeks after the last frost. Corn needs 8–10 inches (20–25 cm) of space between plants and 2.5–3 feet (75–90 cm) of space between rows.

Corn grows best in full sun with at least 8 hours of sunlight per day, but 10 hours is ideal. It's a warm-season crop, and it grows best in temperatures between

85 and 95°F (30–35°C). It needs 1 inch (2.5 cm) of water per week. Corn needs to be fertilized with a balanced liquid fertilizer once the plants are 4 weeks old and then again when the plants are 8–10 weeks old. Corn plants are sturdy and shouldn't need support.

Corn usually takes 90–120 days to grow from seed to harvest, depending on the variety and the weather. Corn is ready for harvest about 20 days after the silk first appears. Corn silk is the long, thread-like strands of plant material that grow underneath the husk of a fresh ear of corn. At harvest time, the silk turns brown, but the husks are still green. When you go to harvest corn, simply take an ear of corn, and bend it downwards and away from the stalk, and it should snap right off. Be careful not to damage the stalk because there might be a few more ears ready to pick in a week or so.

Cucumbers

Cucumbers prefer well-drained soils with pH levels between 6.0 and 7.0.

Cucumbers are annual plants. It's best to sow them directly 1–2 weeks after the last frost. Seeds should be planted 1 inch (2.5 cm) deep. You can start them indoors 3 weeks before planting, and they will transplant OK. Place the cucumber plants outside 2 weeks after the last frost. Cucumbers don't like frost or cold, so don't plant them out too soon. Cucumbers need 3–5 feet (0.9–1.5 m) of space between plants if grown at ground level; however, trellised cucumbers need only 1 foot (30 cm) of space. Rows should be spaced 4–5 feet (1.2–1.5 m) for ground level plants and 1.5–2 feet (45–60 cm) for trellised plants.

Cucumbers like to grow in full sun and need 6–8 hours of sunlight per day. They are a warm-season crop that grows best in temperatures between 75 and 85°F (24–30°C). They need 1–2 inches (2.5–5 cm) of water per week. You can fertilize cucumbers every 3 weeks with a phosphorus- and potassium-rich liquid fertilizer. The main thing cucumbers need to grow well is lots of water. If you think of how much of the inside of a cucumber is water, it's no wonder that they need to be watered regularly. Don't grow cucumbers too large because they can start to taste bitter. Cucumbers can grow on a vine or on a bush. Vines tend to be more common. They have large leaves and will produce an abundant crop. You will need to have a trellis or a fence to support them. Vine varieties can grow 6–8 feet (1.8–2.4 m) tall, and bush varieties can grow 24–36 inches (60–90 cm) tall and wide.

Cucumbers typically take 55–70 days to grow from germination to harvesting. Cucumbers are ready to harvest when they are bright, medium to dark green, and firm. You should avoid harvesting them when they are yellow, puffy, have sunken areas, or wrinkled tips.

Eggplants

Eggplants prefer soil with pH level between 6.0 and 7.0.

Eggplants are biennial plants grown as annuals. They are best started indoors 4–6 weeks before the last frost. Seeds should be planted ¼ to ½ inch (0.6–1.2 cm) deep. You can plant up to two seeds in each cell of a seed starting tray or sow two seeds in each hole directly. Seedlings will be ready to transplant in about 6–8 weeks. They can be transplanted outside 2–3 weeks after the last frost. Eggplants need 18 inches (45 cm) of space between plants and 30–36 inches (75–90 cm) of space between rows.

Eggplants grow best in full sun and need 6–8 hours of sunlight per day. They are a warm-season crop that grows best in temperatures between 70 and 85°F (21–30°C). Eggplants need 1 inch (2.5 cm) of water per week. Eggplants need to be fertilized every 2 weeks with a liquid fertilizer that is high in phosphorus. You can use a balanced fertilizer too. Growing eggplants is similar to growing tomatoes. You don't need to prune eggplants, but doing so will help improve the productivity of your plants. You'll need to remove suckers when the plants are mature. You can also remove yellowing or diseased leaves and branches growing tall and lanky. Eggplant bushes can grow quite tall, so you'll need to tie your plants to a stake.

Eggplants usually take 2–3 months to grow to harvest after transplanting. Harvest eggplants with skin that is glossy and thin. Simply cut a short piece of stem above the cap attached to the top of the fruit with a sharp knife or pruners to harvest them.

Garlic

Garlic prefers well-drained soils with pH levels between 6.0 and 7.0.

Garlic is a perennial crop grown as an annual. It is grown from cloves. Gently separate cloves, and plant them at a depth of 1 inch (2.5 cm) fat end downwards, pointy end up directly in the soil. You would typically plant garlic in March, but it depends on the climate you live in. Garlic should be spaced 6 inches (15 cm) between plants and 10–12 inches (25–30 cm) between rows.

Garlic grows best in full sun, and it needs 6–8 hours of sunlight per day. Garlic is a cool-season crop, and it requires cool air temperatures of 32 to 50°F (0–10°C) during its first 2 months of growth when roots are established and bulbs begin to form. It needs 1 inch (2.5 cm) of water per week during the growing season. You can fertilize garlic in early spring with a liquid fertilizer that is high in nitrogen—blood meal is perfect for garlic. You can fertilize it again when bulbs begin to form, usually in early May.

If you plant garlic in March, you'll need to water it throughout April to June, and you should be able to harvest it in July or August. Garlic is easy to grow, and it has a long growing season. If you have purchased a hardneck (rather than softneck) variety, this will produce a flower that you should remove when it appears so that the energy can go into growing the bulb instead. If you intend to store garlic, leave it to dry for a few days in the sun before storing.

Green Beans

Green beans soils with pH levels between 6.0 and 7.0. If you want to make use of vertical space, then pole beans are a good option. They can grow up fences, stakes, and other support systems. Pole beans will take longer to grow before you're able to harvest them, though. You can also get bush beans which tend to grow 18–24 inches (45–60 cm) in height, and you can usually harvest these within 2 months.

Green beans are annual plants. They don't like being transplanted, so it's best to direct sow them. Sow the seeds 1 inch (2.5 cm) deep just after the last frost. It is best to plant beans in the spring, and they will start to flower 8 weeks later. Bush green beans will grow 2 feet (60 cm) tall and wide, while pole beans can grow anywhere between 6 and 15 feet tall (1.8–5 m) and 2–3 feet (60–90 cm) wide.

Green beans require full sun—they need 6–8 hours of sunlight per day. Ensure that there isn't too much shade where you plant them. Green beans are a warm-season crop that grows best when temperatures range from 65 to 85°F (18–30°C). Green beans need 1–1.5 inches (2.5–3.8 cm) of water per week. They don't need to be fertilized much. Beans enrich the soil with nitrogen themselves, so you can fertilize them with a low-nitrogen liquid fertilizer once a month during the growing season. Pole beans will need a support that is 6–8 feet (1.8–2.4 m) tall, and it's best to have the support in place before planting. Supports should be placed 3–4 feet (0.9–1.2 m) apart.

When beans are the size of a small pencil, they can be harvested, which is typically 50–55 days after planting. They are ready to harvest when the pods are 4–6 inches (10–15 cm) long and slightly firm and before the beans protrude through the skin.

Lettuce

Lettuce prefers well-drained soils with pH levels between 6.0 and 7.0.

Lettuce is an annual plant. Lettuce seeds are small and should be planted ¼ inch (6 mm) deep. I would recommend direct sowing lettuce 2–4 weeks before the last frost. You can also start lettuce indoors 1 month before the last frost and transplant the seedlings outside when they are 2–3 inches (5–7.5 cm) tall. Introduce lettuce seedlings to the outdoors gradually, increasing their time spent outdoors over a week. Spacing will depend on the type of lettuce you're growing. Loose leaf lettuce needs 4 inches (10 cm) of space between plants and 12 inches (30 cm) of space between rows. Romaine lettuce needs 8 inches (20 cm) of space between plants and 12–18 inches (30–45 cm) of space between rows. Iceberg lettuce needs 16 inches (40 cm) of space between plants and 12–18 inches (30–45 cm) of space between rows.

Lettuce needs full or partial sun to grow and at least 5–6 hours of sunlight per day. It grows best in full sun with 8 hours of sunlight per day, though. Lettuce is a cool-season crop that prefers temperatures between 60 and 70°F (15–21°C). It's quite thirsty and will need 1.5–2 inches (3.8–5 cm) of water per week. You can fertilize lettuce every 2 weeks with a balanced liquid fertilizer. Lettuce can keep growing for quite some time—the key requirement is that it gets plenty of water. If the weather is really hot, then lettuce may want some shade in the afternoon.

Lettuce grows fairly quickly. Leaf varieties reach maturity in 30 days, but they can be harvested as soon as they reach the desired size. Other types of lettuce require 6–8 weeks to reach full harvest size. It's best to harvest lettuce in the morning and take young and tender leaves. Always take the outer leaves, and let the inner leaves grow.

Onions

Onions grow best in well-drained soils with pH levels between 6.0 and 7.0.

Onions are biennial plants grown as annuals. You can grow onions from seed or sets. Sets are essentially baby onions. Growing from sets is easier and quicker than growing from seed; however, growing from seed is not difficult. Growing from seed also allows for more choice of variety. You can start seeds indoors 8–10 weeks before the last frost. Sets should be started 6 weeks before the last frost. Plant the seeds about ½ inch (1.2 cm) deep, and water them regularly. Sets should be planted 1–2 inches (2.5–5 cm) deep. You can transplant the seedlings outside 2–4 weeks before the last frost. You can also direct sow seeds 1–2 weeks before the last frost or plant sets 2–4 weeks before the last frost. Onions should be spaced 2–4 inches (5–10 cm) apart with 12–18 inches (30–45 cm) of space between rows.

Onions need full sun. Onions begin to form bulbs when a certain day length is reached. Short-day onion varieties begin to form bulbs when they receive 11 or 12 hours of daylight; intermediate-day (or day-neutral) onions need 12 to 14 hours of daylight, and long-day varieties require 14 or more hours of daylight. Onions are a cool-season crop that grows best in temperatures between 55 and 75°F (13–24°C). They need 1 inch (2.5 cm) of water per week. They need to be fertilized with a liquid fertilizer that's high in nitrogen every 2–3 weeks.

Onions need 90–100 days to grow from seed to harvest. You'll know they're ready to harvest when the leaves droop and turn yellow or brown. Gently loosen the soil around them, and then lift the onions out to harvest them. All varieties of onions will grow green stalks, and you can harvest them 3–4 weeks after planting once they reach 6–8 inches (15–20 cm) in height. Simply cut the largest outer ones, leaving at least an inch (2.5 cm) above the soil. Harvest about a third of the stalks each time.

Peas

Peas prefer well-drained soils with pH levels between 6.0 and 7.0.

Peas are annual plants. I would recommend direct sowing peas 4–6 weeks before the last frost. Seeds should be planted 1–2 inches (2.5–5 cm) deep. You can soak your seeds in water for 24 hours before planting to speed up the germination process. You can also start peas indoors 6–8 weeks before the last frost, and you can transplant the seedlings 4–6 weeks before the last frost. Peas need 2–3 inches (5–7.5 cm) of space between plants and 18 inches (45 cm) of space between rows.

Peas can grow in partial sun, but they grow best in full sun. They need 6–8 hours of sunlight per day. Peas are a cool-season crop that grows best in temperatures between 55 and 65°F (13–18°C). They don't like temperatures over 70°F (21°C). They need 1 inch (2.5 cm) of water per week. Peas don't need lots of fertilizing. Feeding them with a balanced liquid fertilizer every 2–3 weeks is enough. Peas are natural climbers, and they need support to grow in most cases. Bush or dwarf varieties can do without support, but they won't produce a bountiful crop. Vining peas definitely need a trellis—they can grow up to 8 feet (2.4 m) tall. Bush peas can grow 18–30 (45–75 cm) tall and can also benefit from support, especially when they grow over 2 feet (60 cm) tall.

Most varieties of peas need 60–70 days to grow from planting to harvest. Harvest pea pods when they are bright green and noticeably full. They should be plump and swollen.

Peppers

Peppers prefer soils with pH levels between 6.0 and 7.0.

Peppers are perennial plants grown as annuals. They need a lot of warmth and are best started indoors in most climates. You should start them indoors 6–10 weeks before the last frost. For bell peppers, plant the seeds about an inch (2.5 cm) deep, and for chili peppers about ¼ inch (0.6 cm) deep. Seeds will germinate in 1–3 weeks. Transplant the seedlings outside at least

2 weeks after the last frost when they have at least 2 sets of true leaves. Pepper plants need to be spaced 18 inches (45 cm) apart with 30–36 inches (75–90 cm) of space between rows.

Peppers require full sun, and they need at least 6–8 hours of sunlight per day, but they will grow best with up to 12 hours of sunlight per day. Peppers are a warm-season crop that grows best in temperatures between 70 and 80°F (21–27°C). They can grow 3–6 feet (0.9–1.8 m) tall and 18–24 inches (45–60 cm) wide. They need 1–2 inches (2.5–5 cm) of water per week. Peppers need to be fertilized regularly, just like tomatoes. A liquid fertilizer with a lower nitrogen number is perfect, but a balanced fertilizer works well too, and you should use it every 2 weeks. Pepper plants can benefit from having support—stakes and cages are popular options for that. Pinching pepper plants in early stage of their growth will help them become bushier and promote growth. You can pinch pepper plants when they are at least 6 inches (15 cm) tall—simply clip the growing tip. You can also deadhead the flowers if they start appearing too early—this will help direct the plant's energy into growth.

Bell peppers take 2–3 months to be ready for harvesting after transplanting, and chili peppers can take 2–4 months to grow. You can harvest bell peppers when they're green once they reach full size and remain firm. Or you can leave them to ripen, and their color will change into red, yellow, or orange. As for chili peppers, you can harvest them once they reach their mature size and color, but the longer you leave them to ripen, the hotter they will become.

Potatoes

Potatoes prefer well-drained, slightly acidic soils with pH levels between 6 and 6.5, although they can tolerate soils with pH levels as low as 5.

Potatoes are grown from seed potatoes. A seed potato is a potato that is replanted and used to grow more potatoes. You can get them at a garden center or a nursery. Make sure to get ones that are certified and disease-free. You can cut larger seed potatoes (larger than a chicken egg) that have multiple eye buds in half to grow more potatoes. When you're cutting, make sure that each side has at least 2 sprouts. Leave them for a few days after cutting so that the wound can heal, or they will rot otherwise. You can pre-sprout seed potatoes—this will help them develop sprouts, but it's not necessary. It's only required if you live in a climate that has short summers. To pre-sprout your seed potatoes, leave them in a cool, dark place for 2–3 weeks prior to planting.

Potatoes are perennial plants grown as annuals. Plant your seed potatoes 2 weeks after the last frost. They should be planted 6–8 inches (15–20 cm) deep with the majority of the eyes facing upwards and spaced 1 foot (30 cm) apart. After placing the seed potatoes, cover them with soil.

Potatoes grow best in full sun. They ideally need 8 hours of sunlight per day, but they can grow in partial sun too. Potatoes are a cool-season crop, and they grow best in temperatures between 60 and 70°F (15–21°C). They need 1–2 inches of water per week. You can fertilize them with a balanced liquid fertilizer once a month.

Potatoes usually take about 3 months to grow from planting to harvest. Wait until the tops of the vines have yellowed and started to die back before harvesting potatoes.

Pumpkins

Pumpkins prefer well-drained soils with pH levels between 6.0 and 6.8.

Pumpkins are annual plants. I would suggest direct sowing pumpkins 2 weeks after the last frost. Plant the seeds 1 inch (2.5 cm) deep. You can start pumpkin seeds indoors 3–4 weeks before the last frost and transplant them outside 2–3 weeks after the last frost. Pumpkins need to be spaced 2 feet (60 cm) apart with 6–10 feet (1.8–3 m) of space between rows.

Pumpkins need full sun, ideally 8 hours of sunlight per day. Pumpkins are a warm-season crop that grows best in temperatures between 65 and 95°F (18–35°C). They can grow 10–30 inches (25–75 cm) tall and 4–16 feet (1.2–4.8 m) wide, so they will take a lot of space. Pumpkins need 1–2 inches (2.5–5 cm) of water per week. Pumpkins need to be fertilized every 2–3 weeks with a balanced or low-nitrogen liquid fertilizer. Bone meal and compost tea are great for that. Smaller pumpkin varieties will need a strong support, such as an A-shaped trellis.

Pumpkins usually take 3–4 months to grow from planting to harvesting. You can harvest them when they harden and take a uniform and intense color. You can press a pumpkin with your thumb to see if it's ready to be harvested. If the bark is hard and it sounds hollow—it's ready.

Radishes

Radishes prefer well-drained soil with pH level between 6.0 and 7.0.

Radishes can be either annual or biennial plants depending on the variety, but they are grown as annuals. Like with all root crops, it's best to direct sow radishes. You can direct sow them 4–6 weeks before the last frost. Plant the seeds ¼ to ½ an inch (0.6–1.2 cm) deep. Radishes need to be spaced 2–3 inches (5–7.5 cm) apart with 8–12 inches (20–30 cm) of space between rows.

Radishes can grow in full or partial sun. They need at least 6 hours of sunlight per day. Radishes are a cool-season crop that grows best in temperatures between 55 and 65°F (13–18°C). They need 1 inch (2.5 cm) of water per week. Radishes don't need a lot of fertilizing, but you can use a phosphorus-rich liquid fertilizer, such as bone meal, a couple of times during the growing season.

Radishes take 20–70 days to grow from planting to harvesting depending on the variety. Early maturing varieties can be harvested in 20–40 days, while Asian radish varieties take 40–70 days to grow until harvest. A good way to tell if your radishes are ready to be harvested is to simply pull one from the soil. You can harvest them when they're about 1 inch (2.5 cm) in diameter. You can also harvest radish tops. Harvest young and green leaves, and use them in salads and soups.

Spinach

Spinach grows best in well-drained soils with pH levels between 6.5 and 7.

Spinach is an annual crop. You can start spinach indoors 6 weeks before the last frost and transplant it outside right after the last frost. You can also direct sow spinach 4 weeks before the last frost. Plant the seeds ½ inch (1.2 cm) deep. Spinach plants need 2–4 inches (5–10 cm) of space between plants, although some larger varieties may need 3–6 inches (7.5–15 cm) of space. Your seed packet should have information on how much space your particular variety needs. Rows need to be spaced 1 foot (30 cm) apart.

Spinach prefers full sun but can tolerate some shade. It needs at least 4 hours of sunlight per day; however, 4–6 hours is ideal. It's a cool-season crop, and it grows best in temperatures between 50 and 60°F (10–15°C). Spinach needs 1–1.5 inches (2.5–3.8 cm) of water per week. You should fertilize spinach every 2–3 weeks during the growing season with a balanced liquid fertilizer.

Spinach is usually ready for harvest in 6–10 weeks. You can harvest leaves as needed or harvest an entire plant. When the outer leaves are about 6 inches (15 cm) long, they're ready to be harvested. Simply hold each leaf with one hand, and cut the stem with the other one. Harvest no more than a third of a plant at once. If plants are near the end of the season, you can pull up or cut the entire plant.

Tomatoes

Tomatoes prefer well-drained soil with pH level between 6.0 and 6.8. Some tomatoes will grow up to 6 feet (1.8 m) tall, so you will need stakes and maybe a trellis to help grow these up. Another thing to be aware of is how many tomatoes you actually want because all the tomatoes will need to be harvested at the same time, and you'll need to be ready to use them and preserve what you don't want to use immediately. So, it's worth having plenty of mason jars if you plan to grow lots of tomatoes.

Tomatoes can be grown as perennials in their native tropical climate of South and Central America, but they are grown as annuals in other climates. Many people start with seedlings rather than seeds because they take a while to grow. If you decide to purchase seedlings, always get them from a reputable nursery. Plants should be dark green, short, stocky, and have stems the size of a pencil or thicker. They should not have yellow leaves or spots.

If you decide to grow tomatoes from seed, they are almost always started indoors. I would suggest that you start them indoors 6 weeks before the last frost and put the seeds ½ inch (1.2 cm) deep in trays. You can transplant them outside 2 weeks after the last frost. The key warning, though, is not to put them outside too soon because tomatoes love warmth and will not withstand cold weather. Tomato plants need to be spaced 2–3 feet (60–90 cm) apart with 4 feet (1.2 m) of space between rows.

Tomatoes need full sun, ideally at least 8 hours of sunlight per day. Tomatoes are a warm-season crop, and they love warmth. They grow best in temperatures between 70 and 85°F (21–30°C). Before tomatoes start to grow, you will see little yellow flowers. Tomatoes need 1–2 inches (2.5–5 cm) of water per week. They should be first fertilized when you plant them in the garden and then again when they set fruit. After tomato plants start growing fruit, you can fertilize them every 2–3 weeks until harvest. You can get a fertilizer especially formulated for tomatoes, usually with a ratio like 3-4-6 or 4-7-10. You can pinch off small stems and leaves between branches and the main stem. You can stake tomato plants, and I'd recommend doing that, as tomato plants can grow 3–10 feet (0.9–3 m) tall. You can also remove leaves from the bottom 12 inches (30 cm) of the stem.

Tomatoes can be harvested 60–100 days after planting. You can harvest them anytime they've begun to show a bit of color. Bring them indoors, and they'll ripen within a few days.

Zucchini

Zucchini prefer well-drained soils with pH levels between 6.0 and 7.5.

Zucchini are annual plants. Zucchini can be started either indoors or directly in the soil. Zucchini plants have delicate roots and can be difficult to transplant, so I would suggest direct sowing them. You can direct sow them just after the last frost. Plant the seeds 1 inch (2.5 cm) deep. A top tip is to plant zucchini seeds on their sides to reduce the chance of them rotting. You can start them indoors, but you'll have to be careful when transplanting the seedlings so as not to damage their delicate roots. You can start zucchini indoors 4–6 weeks before the last frost and transplant the seedlings outside 1–2 weeks after the last frost. Zucchini plants should be spaced 18–24 inches (45–60 cm) apart with 4 feet (1.2 m) of space between rows.

Zucchini grow best in full sun—they need 6–8 hours of sunlight per day. They are a warm-season crop that grows best in temperatures between 70 and 95°F (21–35°C). They need 1–2 inches (2.5–5 cm) of water per week. Zucchini don't need a lot of fertilizing. You can fertilize them once in the spring and once in the summer with a balanced liquid fertilizer. Zucchini plants can grow up to 2 feet (60 cm) tall and 2–3 feet (60–90 cm) wide. They do not necessarily need support, but they will definitely appreciate it. You can either stake them or get an A-shaped trellis.

Zucchini usually take 45–55 days to grow from seed to harvest. When you come to harvest them, remember that you can eat male zucchini flowers. You can fill and lightly batter them, but remember to leave some of these in order to pollinate the female flowers. Male flowers have a long, thin stem. Female flowers have a swollen base behind the flower—this is the ovary that later develops into a zucchini after germination. When you harvest zucchini, you can cut or twist them off. Smaller zucchini are denser and have a nutty taste. Bigger zucchini are more watery, so don't be tempted to grow your zucchini to a massive size before harvesting them. They taste better when they're smaller.

Fruits

Apples

Apple trees prefer well-drained soils with pH levels between 5.8 and 7.0.

Standard apple trees can grow 25–35 feet (7.5–10 m) tall, but you can get semi-dwarf and dwarf apple trees—they grow 6–20 feet (1.8–6 m) tall. They will bloom and produce apples in the summer or fall. Apple trees need good air circulation so that their leaves can dry and not attract fungus after it has rained. They need to be planted 15 feet (4.5 m) apart. Dwarf varieties can be planted 8 feet (2.4 m) apart.

If you want to grow apple trees from seed, you will have a really long wait—up to 8 years before the trees can bear fruit. Dwarf varieties mature quicker and can bear fruit 2–3 years after planting. You can buy apple trees from a nursery. If you do so, then it's best to buy more than one because most apple trees require another apple tree of a different variety nearby for cross-pollination to produce fruit. You can get self-pollinating apple trees, including dwarf varieties, but they will produce more fruit if another tree is nearby for cross-pollination. It's also important to attract bees to your garden to help with pollination.

Apple trees like to be grown in full sun. They need 1 inch (2.5 cm) of water per week. They need to be fertilized 3 times a year. First, in early spring before flowering, which is around mid-April in most temperate areas. Then you'll need to fertilize them again about a month later after flowering is completed around the end of May. And then, you should fertilize them again about a month after that, around the end of June. You can prune your trees once a year to let in more light and air.

Blueberries

Blueberries like acidic soil with a pH level between 4 and 5.5 pH, and it's best to water them with rainwater rather than tap water (which contains lime and can make soil more alkaline).

You can start blueberry bushes from seed, buy you'll need to be patient—they require a maturation period before fruit production begins. During the first 2 years, it's important to remove blossoms to establish the bush. By year 3, you can expect a bountiful harvest. Alternatively, you can buy an already established plant and propagate more from cuttings.

Blueberry bushes grow up to 4 feet (1.2 m) tall, and they spread to around 3 feet (90 cm). When you plant them, you should ensure they are spaced 5 feet (1.5 m) apart with 10–12 feet (3–3.6 m) of space between rows.

They prefer full sun, but they can grow in partial sun too. They need 6–8 hours of sunlight per day. Blueberries need 1 inch (2.5 cm) of water per week. If you plant two or more of these, they will do better than just a single plant. Blueberry bushes should be fertilized 3 times a year—first in the spring when buds break, then 6 weeks after that, and then again after harvest. Blueberries respond well to any nitrogen-rich fertilizer, but they require fertilizers with an ammonium form of nitrogen, such as cottonseed meal. Any fertilizer sold for azaleas or rhododendrons also works well for blueberries.

For the first couple of years, you shouldn't need to prune blueberries. After this time, you can prune them in February or March and get rid of a quarter of the older branches, keeping the newer ones. When you harvest blueberries, gently pick off the deepest blueberries. If any are green, allow them to fully ripen before picking them off. The more years go by, the greater the harvest you will get from them.

Cherries

Cherry trees prefer well-drained soils with pH levels between 6.0 and 7.0. Standard cherry trees can grow up to 35 feet (10 m) tall, but you can get dwarf varieties that grow 6.5–8 feet (2–2.5 m) tall but still produce full-sized fruit.

You can grow cherry trees from cuttings, seeds, or pits, but it will take years until they mature. They can start producing fruit after 2 years but will reach full cropping between 4 and 5 years, so I would suggest buying a tree from a nursery. There are two main varieties of cherry trees—sweet and sour. Sweet cherries are usually eaten, and sour cherries are typically used for cooking or baking. Sweet cherry trees need to be spaced 35–40 feet (10.7–12.2 m) apart, and their dwarf varieties need 5–10 feet (1.5–3 m) of space. Sour cherry trees need to be spaced 20–25 feet (6–7.6 m) apart, and their dwarf varieties need 8–10 feet (2.4–3 m) of space.

Cherry trees need full sun, ideally 6–8 hours of sunlight per day. Young cherry trees need 2–3 inches (5–7.5 cm) of water every 1–2 weeks, while mature trees only need 1 inch (2.5 cm) of water every 1–2 weeks. Cherry trees don't need a lot of fertilizing—you can use a low-nitrogen fertilizer in the spring 2–3 weeks before the trees blossom. You should prune cherry trees once a year, but try to do it in the warmer months because pruning in the winter makes trees more vulnerable to diseases.

Lemons

Lemon trees prefer well-drained soils with pH levels between 6.0 and 7.5. Lemon trees grow 10–20 feet (3–6 m) tall, but you can get dwarf varieties that stay under 10 feet (3 m) tall, usually 3–5 feet (0.9–1.5 m) tall.

I'd suggest buying lemon trees from a nursery, as it takes 3–6 years to grow a lemon tree from seed to maturity, but you can grow them from cuttings or from seed. If you decide to grow from seed, you could let the seeds dry out for a couple of weeks. Then when they are dry, plant them 1 inch (2.5 cm) deep in a seed starting tray or a container and cover with plastic wrap. Let the seedling get to 10 inches (25 cm) before transplanting it outside. Lemon trees should be spaced 12–25 feet (3.6–7.6 m) apart, while dwarf varieties need to be spaced 6–10 feet (1.8–3 m) apart.

Lemon trees need full sun. They need 8 hours of sunlight to grow. They need 1 inch (2.5 cm) of water per week. Lemon trees should be fertilized with a balanced fertilizer no more than 4 times per year and only when there is active growth, so you can fertilize them from spring right before glowering and until the start of fall. Lemon trees are quite sensitive to the cold, and freezing temperatures can damage or even kill them.

Melons

Melons grow best in well-drained soils, with pH levels between 6.0 and 6.5.

Melons are annual plants. They are best started indoors 4 weeks before the last frost. You can transplant them outside 1 week after the last frost. In warmer climates, you can direct sow melons 1–2 weeks after the last frost. Plant the seeds ½ to 1 inch (1.2–2.5 cm) deep. Melons need 24–36 inches (60–90 cm) of space between plants and 5–6 feet (1.5–1.8 m) of space between rows.

Melons need full sun—at least 8 hours of sunlight per day. They are a warm-season crop, and they grow best in temperatures between 65 and 95°F (18–35°C). Melons need 1–2 inches (2.5–5 cm) of water per week. Melons do best when treated with fertilizer in 2 or 3 applications during the growing season. Phosphorus- and potassium-rich fertilizers are best, but a balanced fertilizer will work fine too.

Melons usually take 80–90 days to grow to maturity after transplanting. Harvest when fruits produce their characteristic melon fragrance and start to crack near the stem. A fully ripe melon will separate from the vine with light pressure. You can also cut melons from the vine with a sharp knife. Leave an inch (2.5 cm) of stem attached to the fruit to keep it from rotting if you don't plan to use the harvested melon immediately.

Peaches and Nectarines

Peach trees prefer well-drained soils with pH levels between 6.0 and 7.0. Unlike apple trees, peach trees have no dwarf rootstock to keep the trees small.

Instead, some varieties naturally grow smaller. They are called natural dwarfs; however, they produce full-sized fruit. They grow 6–10 feet (1.8–3 m) tall. There are also small nectarine trees. Full-sized peach trees should be spaced 15–20 feet (4.5–6 m) apart, and dwarf trees should be spaced 10–12 feet (3–3.6 m) apart.

Like with other fruit trees, I'd suggest getting a tree from a nursery because peach trees can take 3–4 years to mature. They need full sun, ideally 8 hours of sunlight per day. Peach trees need 1–1.5 inches (2.5–3.8 cm) of water per week. You only need to start fertilizing them when they begin bearing fruit, which usually takes 3–4 years. Mature trees should be fertilized twice a year with a balanced fertilizer once in early spring (usually around March) and once in late spring (usually around May). Most peach trees grow compact and don't require pruning. You can prune them if they start getting a bit too large.

Raspberries

Raspberries prefer well-drained soils with pH levels between 5.5 and 6.5.

You can purchase one-year-old raspberry canes from a nursery to plant them. One bush alone can provide you with hundreds of berries in a season. Ideally, you should plant them in the spring, and they will bloom in the summer or fall. It's best to soak the roots of plants for a couple of hours before planting. Raspberry canes should be spaced 18 inches (45 cm) apart with 8–10 feet (2.4–3 m) of space between rows so that you can move freely between them. Rows should be no less than 5 feet (1.5 m) apart because otherwise they'll tend to grow together and create a giant, impenetrable, hard to maintain hedgerow. You can cut the canes down to 9 inches (23 cm) tall after planting, which will encourage new growth. Generally, raspberry bushes will produce fruit a year after you have planted them. You will need to prune the bushes once a year.

Raspberries like to grow in full sun. They need 6–8 hours of sunlight per day. The more sun the bush gets, the more raspberries it will produce. They need 1 inch (2.5 cm) of water per week. You should fertilize them once a year in the spring with a balanced fertilizer. You can also give your raspberry bushes some compost or aged manure every year. They grow 4–8 feet (1.2–2.4 m) tall and 3–5 feet (0.9–1.5 m) wide. You may need supports to keep the canes in place. You could use a trellis or a fence.

After you have harvested your berries, cut the canes that produced them back to the ground. Prune only the old canes (the brown stems that produced berries), and leave the younger green ones. You can tie canes to supports with strings. When it comes to harvesting berries, you'll need to pick them every few days. Try to collect them when it's dry, and you shouldn't need to pull too hard. When they're ripe, it shouldn't be difficult to remove them from the vine.

Strawberries

Strawberries prefer well-drained soils with pH levels between 5.5 and 6.5.

Strawberries are short-term perennials that continuously replicate and renew themselves, and they can be productive for 4–5 years, but they can also be grown as annuals that you replant each year. Strawberries are best started from seed indoors. You can start them indoors 8 weeks before the last frost. Sow the seeds thinly, and press them into the growing medium.

They can take anywhere between 1 and 6 weeks to germinate. You can transplant the seedlings outside after the last frost when they have 3 sets of true leaves. Don't bury the crown when you plant them. The crown should be at the surface of the soil so that it doesn't rot. Strawberries need to be spaced 12–18 inches (30–45 cm) apart with 30 inches (75 cm) of space between rows.

Strawberries like to be grown in full sun. They need 6–8 hours of sunlight per day. They need 1–1.5 inches (2.5–3.8 cm) of water per week. You can fertilize them with a balanced fertilizer once in the spring about a month after you plant them and then again in late summer to early fall. Established strawberries should be fertilized once a year after the final harvest.

When your strawberries bloom depends on what type of strawberry plants you've purchased. If you have got June-bearing strawberries, then you will need to harvest all the fruit in one go over 3 weeks. Everbearing strawberries will produce most of the crop in the spring and some throughout the summer and then another crop in late summer or early fall. Day-neutral varieties will produce fruit all throughout the season until the first frost. I personally like June-bearing strawberries, and while you'll need to wait a year until your first harvest, they taste incredibly delicious, and it's worth the wait.

It is advisable that in the first year you pick off the flowers—this will discourage the plants from fruiting and will help focus their energy on building strong roots instead. This will help you have a bigger yield of berries the following year. If you live in a very cold area, once the strawberries have finished, you can cut the plants down to about an inch (2.5 cm) and place 4 inches (10 cm) of mulch on them. You can remove the mulch in early spring after the last frost.

Herbs

Basil

Basil likes well-drained soils with pH levels between 6.0 and 7.0.

Basil is my favorite herb, and I absolutely adore it. I love the smell, and it's so versatile—it can add such a boost of flavor to many dishes. You can get a variety of flavors of basil: sweet, purple, lemon, and Thai.

Basil is an annual herb. It is best started indoors 6–8 weeks before the last frost. The plant does like warmth, and it won't grow well without it. When you sow basil seeds, put them ¼ inch (0.6 cm) deep. You can transplant the seedlings outside 1–2 weeks after the last frost when they've grown 3 pairs of true leaves. You can also direct sow basil 1–2 weeks after the last frost. Basil plants should be spaced 12 inches (30 cm) apart with at least 18 inches (45 cm) of space between rows.

Basil prefers to grow in full sun with 6–8 hours of sunlight per day, but it can grow in partial shade too. Basil is a warm-season crop that prefers temperatures between 50 and 85°F (10–30°C). It needs 1–1.5 inches (2.5–3.8 cm) of water per week. You can fertilize basil every 3–4 weeks with a balanced liquid fertilizer. If you know there will be a bad frost, harvest basil before this because the cold will destroy basil plants.

Basil usually takes 3–4 weeks to grow from planting to harvest. When the plants are 8 inches (20 cm) tall, they are ready to harvest. It's best to harvest basil in the morning. Picking the leaves will encourage more growth. If you don't need them immediately, you can store them to use when required by freezing or drying the leaves.

Cilantro (Coriander)

Cilantro (coriander) prefers well-drained soils with pH levels between 6.5 and 7.5.

Cilantro (coriander) is an annual herb, although it may survive winter in mild climates. It doesn't like to be transplanted, so it's best to direct sow it after the last frost. Plant the seeds ¼ to ½ inch (0.6–1.2 cm) deep. Cilantro (coriander) plants need to be spaced 6–8 inches (15–20 cm) apart with 12 inches (30 cm) between rows.

Cilantro (coriander) grows best in full sun with 6–8 hours of sunlight per day. It's a cool-season crop, and it grows best in temperatures between 60 and 70°F (15–21°C). It needs 1 inch (2.5 cm) of water per week, and you can fertilize it a couple of times during the growing season with a nitrogen-rich or a balanced liquid fertilizer.

You can harvest the leaves when the plants are at least 6 inches (15 cm) tall, which typically occurs about a month after sowing seeds. Don't harvest more than a third of the leaves at a time. If you want to harvest seeds, you'll need to let your plants flower, which can take around 100 days from sowing seeds. To harvest seeds, leaves seed heads on your plants to dry out, and then shake them into a paper bag to release the seeds, or you can snip the entire seedhead, place it into a paper bag, put the bag in a cool, dark, well-ventilated place, and allow the seeds to finish drying in the bag for easier harvest.

Dill

Dill prefers well-drained soils with pH levels between 5.5 and 6.5.

Dill is an annual herb. It doesn't transplant well, so it's best to direct sow it. You can sow the seeds ¼ inch (0.6 cm) deep after the last frost. Dill plants should be spaced 10–12 inches (25–30 cm) apart with 2–3 feet (60–90 cm) of space between rows.

Dill grows best in full sun with 6–8 hours of sunlight per day. It's a cool-season crop, and it grows best in temperatures between 60 and 70°F (15–21°C). Dill needs 1 inch (2.5 cm) of water per week. It doesn't need a lot of fertilizing. A light feeding of a phosphorus-rich or a balanced liquid fertilizer applied once in late spring should be enough.

Dill is usually ready for harvest 90 days after planting. To harvest, snip the stems of the leaves right where they meet the growth point on the main stem with a pair of scissors.

Oregano

Oregano prefers well-drained soils with pH levels between 6.0 and 8.0.

Oregano is a hardy perennial herb, but it prefers warmer climates. You can start oregano indoors 4 weeks before the last frost. Plant the seeds ¼ inch (0.6 cm) deep. For some varieties, you don't need to cover the seeds with soil—you can simply sprinkle them on the surface of the soil. Your seed packet should have information on how deep the seeds should be planted. You can transplant the seedlings outside 1–2 weeks after the last frost. You can also sow it directly after the last frost. Oregano plants need to be spaced 12 inches (30 cm) apart with 18 inches (45 cm) of space between rows.

Oregano prefers to grow in full sun with 6–8 hours of sunlight per day. The more sun it gets, the stronger the flavor will be. It grows best in temperatures between 60 and 80°F (15–27°C). Oregano needs 1 inch (2.5 cm) of water per week. It typically doesn't need a lot of fertilizing. If you added compost to your garden beds, you won't need to do much else in terms of fertilizing. If you have a bushier plant, you can prune it once it's at least 4 inches (10 cm) tall. Pinch the top part along with the first set of leaves just above the leaf node. This will make your plant grow thick and lush.

Oregano usually takes 45 days to grow from planting to harvesting. You can start harvesting leaves as needed once the plant is at least 6 inches (15 cm) tall. Never harvest more than ⅔ of all leaves. Oregano loses flavor after flowering, so it's best to harvest it before that.

Parsley

Parsley prefers well-drained soils with pH levels between 6.0 and 7.0.

Parsley is a biennial herb grown as an annual. You can start parsley indoors or direct sow it. You can start it indoors 6–10 weeks before the last frost. Soaking the seeds in water for 12–24 hours before planting can help with germination. Plant the seeds ¼ inch (0.6 cm) deep. They can be a bit finicky, so you can plant 2–3 seeds in each seed starting tray cell or container. Parsley is frost hardy, so you can move it outside 2–4 weeks before the last frost, or you can wait until after the last frost, just in case. You can also direct sow it 3–4 weeks before the last frost. Parsley plants need to be spaced 6–8 inches (15–20 cm) apart with rows 12–18 inches (30–45 cm) apart.

Parsley grows well in full or partial sun. It needs at least 6 hours of sunlight per day. It's a hardy herb, and it grows best in temperatures between 50 and 70°F (10–21°C). Parsley needs 1–2 inches (2.5–5 cm) of water per week. It doesn't need a lot of fertilizing. You can fertilize it every 4–6 weeks during the growing season with a balanced or phosphorus-rich liquid fertilizer. You can remove the flower stalks, and this should help the plant focus on foliage growth instead. You can also pick dead, faded, and yellowed leaves from time to time.

Parsley typically takes 70–90 days to grow from planting to harvest. You can start harvesting parsley leaves as needed 2–3 months after planting. Wait until the stems are divided into three sections before harvesting. Instead of only picking the leaves from the top, cut the entire stem carefully from the base—parsley stems are also edible and tasty.

Rosemary

Rosemary prefers soils with pH levels between 6.0 and 7.0.

Rosemary is a perennial shrub, but it prefers warmer climates. It is rather difficult to grow from seed. The germination rate is quite low, and it will take months until the plant can produce usable leaves. It's much easier to grow rosemary from cuttings, so I'd suggest getting a plant from a nursery and then propagating it via cuttings.

If you decide to grow it from seed, I would recommend that you start them indoors. You can start them indoors 10 weeks before the last frost. Plant the seeds ¼ inch (0.6 cm) deep. You can transplant the seedlings outside 1–2 weeks after the last frost. Rosemary plants need to be spaced 1.5–3 feet (45–90 cm) apart with 1.5–2 feet (45–60 cm) of space between rows.

Rosemary likes to grow in full sun with 6–8 hours of sunlight per day. It grows best in temperatures between 60 and 80°F (15–27°C). It needs 1 inch (2.5 cm) of water every 1–2 weeks. Rosemary doesn't like sitting in moist or wet soil, so water it only when the top 2 inches (5 cm) of the soil are dry. Rosemary doesn't need a lot of fertilizing. You can fertilize it with a balanced liquid fertilizer once a month during the growing season. You can cut the plants back if they start to become woody.

Rosemary takes 80–100 days to grow from planting to harvest if you grow it from cuttings. If you grow it from seed, it can take a year to grow to maturity. You can harvest rosemary by pulling sprigs off the main stem. If you need large branches to roast, then you could use secateurs to remove these. You can dry rosemary, but you can't freeze it.

Sage

Sage prefers well-drained soils with pH levels between 6.0 and 7.0.

Sage can be an annual or a perennial herb depending on your climate. It can be grown as a perennial in colder to moderate climates and as an annual in hotter climates. You can grow sage from seed, but just like rosemary, sage is rather difficult to grow from seed. I'd suggest getting a plant from a nursery and then propagating it via cuttings.

If you decide to grow it from seed, I would recommend starting them indoors 6–8 weeks before the last frost. Plant the seeds ⅛ inch (3 mm) deep. You can transplant the seedlings outside 1–2 weeks after the last frost. Sage plants need to be spaced 12–18 inches (30–45 cm) apart with 18 inches (45 cm) of space between rows.

Sage is an herb that likes to be grown in full sun with 6–8 hours of sunlight per day. It grows best in temperatures between 60 and 70°F (15–21°C). Sage needs 1 inch (2.5 cm) of water per week. It doesn't need a lot of fertilizing. In fact, overfertilizing it can result in weaker flavor. You can use a balanced liquid fertilizer every 4–6 weeks during the growing season. If the plants become woody, you can prune them. You need to give sage plants a good pruning every year. It's best to do it when new growth starts to appear, young leaves unfurl, and new buds form in the spring. Sage plants need to be replaced every couple of years to remain productive.

Sage typically takes 75 days to grow from cuttings to harvest. To harvest sage, you can pinch off some leaves or sprigs from it. Try not to harvest too much from the plants in the first year. When the plants are fully established, you can harvest them 3 times in a growing season. Don't harvest them in the fall so that the plants can prepare for winter. Fresh sage tastes best, but you can freeze or dry it. If you're drying it, hang sprigs in a warm area and allow to air dry.

Thyme

Thyme prefers well-drained soils with pH levels between 6.0 and 8.0.

Thyme is a perennial herb. You can grow thyme from seed or cuttings. You can start it indoors 6–10 weeks before the last frost. Plant the seeds ¼ inch (0.6 cm) deep. You can transplant the seedlings outside after the last frost. You can also direct sow it after the last frost. Or you can save yourself the hassle of growing from seed and get a plant from a nursery and then propagate it via cuttings. Thyme plants need to be spaced 12–24 inches (30–60 cm) apart with 18–24 inches (45–60 cm) of space between rows.

Thyme prefers to grow in full sun with 6–8 hours of sunlight per day. It grows best in temperatures between 65 and 85°F (18–30°C). It's an herb that doesn't need too much water. It only needs 1 inch (2.5 cm) of water every 10–15 days. Thyme doesn't need a lot of fertilizing. You can fertilize it with a balanced liquid fertilizer every 6–8 weeks during the growing season. Just like rosemary, thyme likes dry conditions, so you can grow them together. You can prune thyme back in the spring and summer. If you've had the plants for 3–4 years, you may want to replace them, as they may not taste as flavorful.

You can harvest thyme all year round, but to get the most flavor, harvest it just before it starts flowering. Cut only a few stems in the first year. Many gardeners don't harvest thyme in the first year at all. It's best to cut off the top 5–6 inches (12.5–15 cm) when you harvest this and do it in the morning. Don't wash it because doing so will remove the essential oils. You can freeze it or dry the leaves in the oven or by hanging them.

Flowers

Marigolds

Marigolds prefer well-drained soils with pH levels between 6.0 and 7.5.

Most marigolds are annuals, but some varieties are perennials. Most varieties of marigolds are self-seeding, so they may appear to be perennials, but in reality, they are just coming back from seed. Marigold seeds are easy to germinate, so there is really no advantage to starting them indoors. You can direct sow them 1–2 weeks after the last frost, and they will bloom in 8 weeks. Plant the seeds ⅛ inch (3 mm) deep. French marigolds need to be spaced 8–10 inches (20–25 cm) apart, and African marigolds need 10–12 inches (25–30 cm) of space between plants.

Marigolds are a beautiful, vibrant orange color, and they are an asset to any garden. They've been mentioned a few times in this book, and for a good reason. They are a perfect companion plant for pretty much any crop because they grow well with everything, and they help repel pests and attract pollinators and beneficial insects, such as butterflies, bees, and ladybugs.

Marigolds can grow in full or partial sun. They need 5–6 hours of sunlight per day. Marigolds grow best in temperature between 65 and 75°F (18–24°C). They need around 1.5 inches (3.8 cm) of water per week. They typically don't need fertilizing, especially if your soil has been enriched with compost. They typically grow 6–18 inches (15–45 cm) tall. They will bloom from late spring and until fall. You can deadhead marigolds flowers, which will make the plant look better and encourage further growth.

There is a wide variety of marigolds available all in warm, sunny colors. They can be from 6 inches (15 cm) to 4 feet (15 cm–1.2 m) tall and from 6 inches (15 cm) to 2 feet (15–60 cm) wide. French marigolds are the most common type. There are also tall African marigolds and Signet marigolds, which are edible and can be used in salads and pastas. If you're growing the taller African marigolds, you should plant them in early spring after the last frost because they take longer to grow and mature. But other types can be planted any time in the spring or summer. The taller varieties need to be protected from strong winds and may need a support stake.

Nasturtiums

Nasturtiums prefer well-drained soils with pH levels between 6.0 and 8.0.

Nasturtiums are an annual plant. They are best sown directly because they have delicate roots and don't transplant well. You can sow them directly 1–2 weeks after the last frost. Plant the seeds ¼ to ½ inch (0.6–1.2 cm) deep. Nasturtiums need to be spaced 10–12 inches (25–30 cm) apart with at least 12 inches (30 cm) of space between rows.

Nasturtiums do best in full sun. They need 6–8 hours of sunlight per day. Nasturtiums grow best in temperatures between 60 and 75°F (15–24°C). They need 1 inch (2.5 cm) of water per week. They don't need to be fertilized. If you fertilize them, it will increase foliage growth but won't help increase flower growth. They are fast growing and easy to look after.

There are many different types of nasturtiums, including bushy plants, trailing plants, and climbers, so if you like these, you can add a variety of different types to your garden. The leaves and flowers are edible, and they have a peppery taste. Depending on the type you buy, they can be 1–10 feet (30 cm–3 m) tall, and 1–3 feet (30–90 cm) wide. They bloom from May to September.

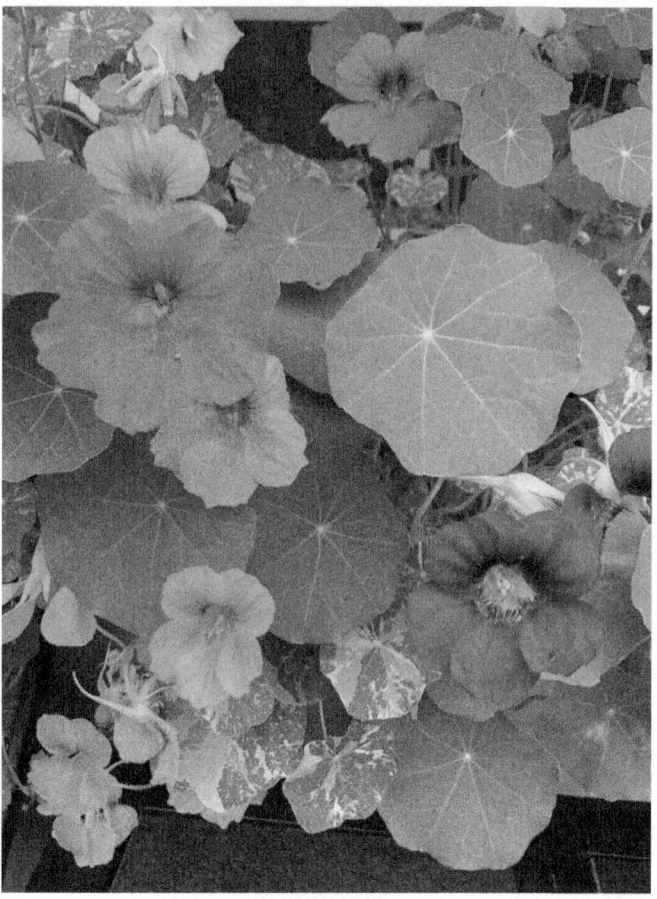

My personal favorite plants to grow are tomatoes. I just think they're incredibly versatile. They're tangy, sweet, and have a rich taste. You can use them in salads, eat them as a snack, make soups out of them, and make delicious sauces for pizzas, pastas, and other dishes. But I also love the great variety of vegetables, fruits, herbs, and flowers that we grow. They all bring something to our table in terms of flavor, great nutrition, vitamins, and help us live a healthy, organic, and sustainable lifestyle.

Key takeaways from this chapter:

1. Whether buying seeds or seedlings, be certain to check all plant information thoroughly to see how big the plants grow, what sun requirements they have, what soil type they prefer, when to plant them, how deep to plant the seeds, how far apart you should space them, and when to prune them.
2. You may need to thin seedlings out to give the strongest ones room to grow.
3. Some plants, such as carrots, don't like to be transplanted, so it's best to sow them directly. Other plants may need to be grown indoors and then transplanted outside when ready—check this before purchasing.
4. You may need to provide support for climbing plants or plants that grow tall. You can use stakes, canes, fences, or trellises to provide support for plants that need it.
5. Many vegetables and fruits taste better when they're smaller, so there's no need to grow them to a huge size.
6. Remember that dwarf varieties of plants and trees are a great option if you don't have a lot of space.
7. Some plants, like sage, will need to be replaced after a few years because they won't be as flavorful with time.

Conclusion

No-till gardening has numerous benefits that make it so worthwhile, from improving your soil quality and fertility to helping your plants to be healthier, all with less hard work and heavy machinery usage. No-till gardening makes the soil richer and more sustainable in the long term and helps plants get the nutrients they need. By using no-till techniques, you can grow vegetables organically without the need for chemical fertilizers or pesticides. Your garden will have a more varied beautiful appearance being interspersed with vibrant, colorful, and amazing smelling vegetables, fruits, herbs, and flowers. Your garden will thrive with beneficial insects and pollinators, which will give you healthier plants and generally be much better for the environment. There's nothing not to love about no-till gardening. I truly hope that you get as much pleasure from it as I do.

This book has outlined the many benefits of no-till gardening in Chapter 1. Chapter 2 covered how you can pick the perfect location for your garden and when to plant it. Chapter 3 gave detailed information about starting your no-till garden from scratch as well as transitioning to no-till if you have an existing garden, plus it covered building raised beds in case you'd prefer to go that route. Chapter 4 focused on how you could start your garden, and it looked at starting plants from seed and growing seedlings as well propagating plants from cuttings. Chapter 5 covered the necessary maintenance of your garden, including watering, mulching, weeding, pruning plants, and providing support for plants that need it. Chapter 6 gave information on soil fertility management, covering techniques such as fertilizing, making and using compost, cover cropping, and crop rotation, all of which will help maintain and improve your soil fertility in the long term. Chapter 7 focused on pest control and dealing with diseases using organic options, using trap crops for pest control, attracting beneficial insects, and it emphasized the importance of preventing diseases from the outset. Chapter 8 looked at harvesting the bounty from your vegetable garden, looking at how you know when to harvest, how to do this safely to not damage plants, and how to store your produce to keep it fresh. Finally, Chapter 9 covered plant profiles to provide you information about the plants you might want to grow so that you have a good indication as to their sun requirements, whether they're better started indoors or sown directly, how much water they require, how often they should be fertilized, and more.

This concludes the end of this book. I think it's a really exciting topic that you can constantly work upon to improve your soil quality and your garden so that you can grow delicious produce to make a sustainable life for you and your family for generations to come.

I'm sure there are lots of things you can be doing, whether that's planning out your garden, ordering seeds, starting seeds or planting out seedlings, weeding, watering, observing your garden to make sure your plants don't have any pests or diseases, or gathering your harvest. Have a wonderful time, and most importantly, enjoy it!

Resources

No-Till Gardening

Frost, Jesse. 2018. Four Basic Principles of No-Till Growing. *No-Till Growers*. Online. 27 November 2018.
https://www.notillgrowers.com/blog/2018/11/27/the-four-basic-priciples-of-no-till-market-gardening

Hailey, Logan. 2023. 11 Benefits of No-Till Gardening. *Epic Gardening*. Online 25 September 2023.
https://www.epicgardening.com/benefits-of-no-till-gardening/

Kellogg Biological Station | Long-Term Ecological Research. Long-term data reveals how no-till agriculture increases crop yields and environmental gains over the long haul. Online. 18 May 2020.
https://lter.kbs.msu.edu/2020/05/no-till-agriculture-increases-crop-yields-environmental-gains-over-long-haul/#:~:text=Scientists%20know%20that%20yields%20from,higher%20percentage%20of%20organic%20matter

Seaman, Greg. 2022. No-Till Gardening. *Eartheasy*. Online. 28 February 2022.
https://learn.eartheasy.com/articles/no-till-gardening/

Choosing the Perfect Location for Your Garden

Almanac. 2021. Where to Put a Vegetable Garden. Online. *Almanac*. 21st December 2021.
https://www.almanac.com/where-put-vegetable-garden

Andrychowicz, Amy. 2022. How Much Sunlight Does my Garden Get – The Ultimate Sun Exposure Guide. *Get Busy Gardening*. Online.
https://getbusygardening.com/how-to-determine-sun-exposure/

MLGG. 2022. How to Determine the Best Sun Exposure for Your Garden. *My Little Green Garden*. Online. 28th May 2022.
https://mylittlegreengarden.com/sun-exposure-for-your-garden/

Neveln, Viveka. 2020. How to Understand Your Yard's Sunlight so you Know What to Plant Where. Online. 1st June 2020.
https://www.bhg.com/gardening/how-to-garden/understanding-your-yard-s-sunlight/

Poindexter, Jennifer. 2022. 12 Steps to Choosing the Best Location for Your Vegetable Garden. *Morning Chores*. Online.
https://morningchores.com/vegetable-garden-location/

Organic Gardening

Rinkesh. 2022. What is Organic Gardening? *Conserve Energy Future*. Online.
https://www.conserve-energy-future.com/start-an-organic-garden.php

SaferBrand. 2022. Why Choose Organic Gardening? *Safer Brand*. Online.
https://www.saferbrand.com/advice/organic-gardening/why-organic

Yares, Kat. 2021. Five Benefits of Growing an Organic Garden. *Gardening Know How*. Online. 14th June 2021.
https://www.gardeningknowhow.com/special/organic/five-benefits-of-growing-an-organic-garden.htm

Starting a No-Till Garden from Scratch/Transitioning to No-Till

Collie, Sarah. 2023. Want Healthier and More Productive Plants? Transition Your Garden to No-Till in 7 Easy Steps. *Seeds'n'Such*. Online. 27 March 2023.
https://seedsnsuch.com/blogs/gardeners-greenroom/no-till

Garden Organic. N.d. The No-Dig Method. *Garden Organic*. Online.
https://www.gardenorganic.org.uk/no-dig-method

Mitchel-Pollock, Margarita. 2021. No dig gardening: The 7 layers of a no dig garden explained. *CountryLiving*. Online. 28th August 2021.

https://www.countryliving.com/uk/homes-interiors/gardens/a37393447/no-dig-gardening-method/

Sass, Neil. 2019. 6 Tips for Switching to No-Till. *USDA*. Online. 20 November 2019.

https://www.farmers.gov/blog/6-tips-switching-no-till

Sowards, Jessica. 2022. No-Till Gardening (The Various Methods). *Roots & Refuge*. Online. 3 June 2022.

https://rootsandrefuge.com/no-till-gardening-the-various-methods/

Sunshine Farm. 2021. How to Start a No-Till Garden from Scratch. *Sunshine Farm*. Online. 11 May 2021.

https://sunshinefarmny.com/2021/05/11/how-to-start-a-no-till-garden-from-scratch/

Raised Beds

Almanac. 2022. A Step-by-Step Guide to Building an Easy DIY Raised Garden Bed. *Almanac*. Online. 26th May 2022.

https://www.almanac.com/content/how-build-raised-garden-bed

Gardener's Supply Company. 2022. The Basics: Gardening in Raised Beds. *Gardener's Supply Company*. 3rd March 2022. Online.

https://www.gardeners.com/how-to/raised-bed-basics/8565.html

Margaret. 2021. How to Water Raised Beds: The Complete Guide. Online. *Crate & Basket*.

https://crateandbasket.com/how-to-water-raised-beds/

Seeding and Transplanting

Borchert, Mikayla. 2021. When is the Best Time to Start Growing a Garden? *Family Handyman*. Online. 13th September 2021.

https://www.familyhandyman.com/article/when-to-start-a-garden/

Collier, Sommer. 2014. Selecting Your Seeds. *A Spicy Perspective*. Online. 13th March 2014.

https://www.aspicyperspective.com/select-seeds/

Gardener's Supply Company. 2022. How to Start Seeds. *Gardener's Supply Company*. 15th February 2022. Online.

https://www.gardeners.com/how-to/how-to-start-seeds/5062.html

Harlow, Ivory. 2015. How to Transplant Vegetable Seedlings. *Farm and Dairy*. Online. 15th May 2015. https://www.farmanddairy.com/top-stories/how-to-transplant-vegetable-seedlings/258509.html

Iannotti, Marie. 2022. How to Start Seeds Indoors. *The Spruce*. Online. 14th June 2022.

https://www.thespruce.com/successful-start-seed-indoors-1402478

Sparks, Madaline. 2022. When to Start Planting Vegetables in Your Garden, a Month-by-Month Guide. *RealSimple*. Online. 28th April 2022.

https://www.realsimple.com/home-organizing/gardening/outdoor/month-by-month-vegetable-gardening-guide

Maintaining Your Garden

Harrington, Jenny. N.d. Steps to Take Care of a Vegetable Garden. *SFGate*. Online.

https://homeguides.sfgate.com/steps-care-vegetable-garden-68300.html

Ianotti, Marie. 2021. How to Take Care of a Vegetable Garden. *The Spruce*. Online 14th November 2021. https://www.thespruce.com/vegetable-garden-maintenance-1403170

MacKenzi, Jill. 2018. Watering the Vegetable Garden. *University of Minnesota Extension*. Online.

https://extension.umn.edu/water-wisely-start-your-own-backyard/watering-vegetable-garden

Tilley, Nikki. 2021. Watering the Garden – Tips on How and When to Water the Garden. *Gardening Know How*. Online. 25th June 2021.

https://www.gardeningknowhow.com/garden-how-to/watering/watering-garden.htm

Weed Control

Burke, Kelly. 2022. Organic Methods for Killing Weeds Safely. *The Spruce*. Online. 16th March 2022. https://www.thespruce.com/green-weed-killers-2152938

Muntean, Laura. 2021. How to manage garden weeds with mulch. *Agrilife Today*. 26th March 2021. Online.

https://agrilifetoday.tamu.edu/2021/03/26/how-to-manage-garden-weeds-with-mulch/

Walliser, Jessica. 2017. Organic weed control tips for gardeners. *Savvy Gardening*. Online. https://savvygardening.com/organic-weed-control-tips/

Compost

Beck, Andrea. 2022. Your Step-by-Step Guide on How to Make Compost to Enrich Your Garden. *Better Homes and Gardens*. Online. 13th May 2022.

https://www.bhg.com/gardening/yard/compost/how-to-compost/

Ellis, Mary Ellen. 2021. What to do With Compost – Learn About Compost Uses in the Garden. *Gardening Know How*. Online. 27th December 2021.

https://www.gardeningknowhow.com/composting/basics/what-to-do-with-compost.htm

Jeanroy, Amy. 2022. How to Make Your Own Compost. *The Spruce*. Online 23rd March 2022.

https://www.thespruce.com/how-to-make-compost-p2-1761841

Soil Fertility Management

Pleasant, Barbara. 2020. Use Cover Crops to Improve Soil. *MotherEarthNews*. Online. 7th July 2020.

https://www.motherearthnews.com/organic-gardening/cover-crops-improve-soil-zmaz09onzraw/

Rhoades, Heather. 2022. Improving Compacted Soil – What to Do When Soil is Too Compact. *Gardening Know How*. Online.

https://www.gardeningknowhow.com/garden-how-to/soil-fertilizers/improving-compacted-soil.htm

Salisbury. 2021. Crop Rotation is the Key to Breaking Disease Cycles. Online.

https://salisburygreenhouse.com/crop-rotation-is-the-key-to-breaking-disease-cycles/

Fertilizing

All That Grows. 2022. Organic Fertilizers: Everything You Need to Know. *All That Grows*. Online.

https://www.allthatgrows.in/blogs/posts/organic-fertilizers

Cary, Bill. 2022. When and how to add organic fertilizers to your soil. *Lohud*. Online.

https://eu.lohud.com/story/life/home-garden/in-the-garden/2014/05/01/add-organic-fertilizers/8578063/

Pennington. 2022. All You Need to Know About Organic Fertilizer. *Pennington*. Online.

https://www.pennington.com/all-products/fertilizer/resources/what-is-organic-fertilizer

Companion Planting

Almanac. 2022. Companion Planting Guide for Vegetables. *Almanac*. 26th May 2022.

https://www.almanac.com/companion-planting-guide-vegetables

Hassani, Nadia. 2021. What is Companion Planting? A Guide to Companion Planting in Your Vegetable Garden. *The Spruce*. Online. 29th November 2021. https://www.thespruce.com/companion-planting-with-chart-5025124

Hicks-Hamblin, Kristina. 2021. The Scientifically-Backed Benefits of Companion Planting. *Gardener's Path*. 29th September 2021. Online. https://gardenerspath.com/how-to/organic/benefits-companion-planting/

Pest Control

Dekker, Sylvia. 2022. How to Use Trap Crops as Decoys to Control Insect Pests. *Gardener's Path*. Online. 26th February 2022.

https://gardenerspath.com/how-to/disease-and-pests/trap-crop-decoys/

Herring, Barbara, 2018. 10 Common Garden Pests – and Natural Pesticides to Keep Them Away. *Eco Warrior Princess*. Online. 29th January 2018. https://ecowarriorprincess.net/2018/01/10-common-garden-pests-and-natural-pesticides-to-keep-them-away/

Ianotti, Marie. 2020. Companion Planting to Control the Insects in Your Garden. *The Spruce*. Online. 21st October 2020.

https://www.thespruce.com/companion-planting-1402735

Johnson, Scott. 2022. Organic Pest Control for Your Garden That Really Works. Online. 4th January 2022. *Lawn Starter*.

https://www.lawnstarter.com/blog/gardening-2/organic-pest-control-that-works/

Miller, Carley. 2022. 21 Companion Plants for Pest Control. *Bustling Nest*. Online.
https://bustlingnest.com/companion-plants-for-pest-control/

Organic Lesson. 2018. 14 Beneficial Insects for Natural Garden Pest Control. *Organic Lesson*. 26th February 2018. Online.

https://www.organiclesson.com/beneficial-insects-garden-pest-control/

Sim, Adriana. 2022. Organic Pest Control Methods for Your Vegetable Garden. *Tiny Garden Habit*. Online. https://www.tinygardenhabit.com/organic-pest-control-methods-for-your-vegetable-garden/

Walliser, Jessica. 2017. Guide to Vegetable Garden Pests: Identification and Organic Controls. *Savvy Gardening*. Online. https://savvygardening.com/guide-to-vegetable-garden-pests/

Disease Management

Poindexter, Jennifer. 2022. Most Common Vegetable Garden Diseases and Solutions. *Clean Air Gardening*. Online.

https://www.cleanairgardening.com/most-common-vegetable-garden-diseases-and-solutions/

Smith, Cheryl. 2022. 10 Easy Steps to Prevent Common Garden Diseases [fact sheet], *University of New Hampshire*. Online.

https://extension.unh.edu/resource/10-easy-steps-prevent-common-garden-diseases-fact-sheet

The Big Greenk. 2022. 5 Common Garden Vegetable Diseases. *The Big Greenk*. Online. 1st February 2022.

https://thebiggreenk.com/blog/5-common-garden-vegetable-diseases/

University of Georgia Extension. 2020. Disease Management in the Home Vegetable Garden. *University of Georgia Extension*. Online.

https://extension.uga.edu/publications/detail.html?number=C862&title=Disease%20Management%20in%20the%20Home%20Vegetable%20Garden

Vanderlinden, Colleen. 2022. Preventing Plant Diseases with Good Gardening Practices. *The Spruce*. Online. 16th May 2022.

https://www.thespruce.com/prevent-plant-diseases-in-your-garden-2539511

Attracting Beneficial Garden Insects and Pollinators

Hoffman, Fred. 2014. Plants that attract beneficial insects. *Permaculture News*. Online. 4th October 2014. https://www.permaculturenews.org/2014/10/04/plants-attract-beneficial-insects/

Ianotti, Marie. 2022. How to Attract Bees and Other Pollinators to Your Garden. *The Spruce*. Online. 18th March 2022. https://www.thespruce.com/bee-plants-1401948

Harvesting and Storing Your Produce

Chadwick, Pat. 2020. Guidelines for Harvesting Vegetables. *Piedmont Master Gardeners*. Online. https://piedmontmastergardeners.org/article/guidelines-for-harvesting-vegetables/

Ianotti, Marie. 2020. When and How to Harvest Garden Vegetables. *The Spruce*. Online. 17th September 2020. https://www.thespruce.com/when-to-harvest-vegetables-1403402

Poindexter, Jennifer. 2022. How to Store Your Garden Harvest Properly to Keep It Fresh Longer. *Morning Chores*. Online. https://morningchores.com/how-to-store-your-harvest/

Tong, Cindy. 2021. Harvesting and storing home garden vegetables. *University of Minnesota Extension*. Online. https://extension.umn.edu/planting-and-growing-guides/harvesting-and-storing-home-garden-vegetables

Plant Profiles

Almanac. 2022. Growing Guides. *Almanac*. Online. https://www.almanac.com/gardening/growing-guides

Garden Design. 2022. 21 Easy Flowers for Beginners to Grow *Garden Design*. Online. https://www.gardendesign.com/flowers/easy.html

Index

A

anthracnose, 85
ants, 72
aphids, 71
apple trees, 115
attracting beneficial insects, 81

B

Bacillus thuringiensis (Bt), 82
Bacillus thuringiensis kurstaki (Btk), 82
Bacillus thuringiensis var. san diego (Bt var. san diego), 82
bacterial diseases, 89
bacterial leaf spot, 89
bacterial soft rot, 90
basil, 119
beets (beetroot), 104
beneficial insects, 81
birds, 72
black rot, 90
black spot, 85
blight, 85
blossom-end rot, 91
blueberries, 116
broccoli, 105
buckwheat, 66
building raised beds, 33

C

cabbage, 105
cabbage worms, 72
carrot rust flies, 72
carrots, 106
caterpillars, 73
cauliflower, 106
celery, 106
cereal rye, 67
checking and changing soil pH level, 35
cherry trees, 116
choosing the perfect location for your garden, 14
cilantro (coriander), 120
clubroot, 86
codling moths, 73
collard greens, 107
colorado potato beetles, 73
common garden pests, 71
common plant diseases, 84
companion planting, 64
companion planting for disease management, 93
companion planting for pest control, 64
compost, 62
contact weed killers, 53
corn, 107
cover cropping, 66
cover crops, 66
crimson clover, 67
crop rotation, 67
cucumber beetles, 73
cucumbers, 108
cutworms, 74

D

damping off, 41, 86
dappled sun/shade, 17
deadheading plants, 55
dealing with diseases, 84
determining when to plant your garden, 18
diatomaceous earth, 80
dill, 120
direct sowing, 38
disease prevention, 92
downy mildew, 86
drip irrigation for in-ground gardens, 50
drip irrigation for raised beds, 50

E

eggplants, 108
evaluating sun requirements and exposure, 17

F

fennel, 65
fertilizing, 60
filling raised beds, 34
flea beetles, 74
full shade, 17
full sun, 17

fungal diseases, 84
fungicides (organic), 84

G

gardening tools, 21
garlic, 109
gray mold, 87
green beans, 109
grow lights for starting seeds, 40
growing seedlings, 41

H

half-hardy crops, 20
hand weeding, 52
hardy crops, 20
harvesting, 95
homemade organic fertilizers, 61
homemade organic fungicides, 84
homemade organic pesticides, 79

I

insecticidal soap, 79
intercropping, 64
issues with seeds, 40

L

lacewings, 82
ladybugs, 82
last frost date, 19

leaf miners, 74
lemon trees, 117
lettuce, 110

M

maintaining your garden, 53
making compost, 62
marigolds, 64, 76, 83, 123
mealybugs, 75
melons, 117
mexican nean neetles, 75
mosaic virus, 90
mulching, 51
mustard, 67, 83

N

nasturtiums, 65, 83, 124
nectarine trees, 117
neem oil, 79
no-dig gardening method, 26
no-till gardening basics, 9
no-till gardening benefits, 11
no-till gardening principles, 9

O

oilseed radish, 67
onions, 110
oregano, 120
organic fertilizers, 60
organic seeds, 37

P

parsley, 121

partial shade (or part shade), 17
peach trees, 117
peas, 111
peppers, 111
pest control, 78
pesticides (organic), 79
pill bugs, 75
pinching plants, 55
planning your garden, 14
plant families, 68
plant growth stages, 53
plant profiles, 104
potatoes, 112
powdery mildew, 88
preventing animals from eating plants, 56
propagating plants from cuttings, 44
pruning plants, 55
pumpkins, 113

R

radishes, 83, 113
raised beds, 31
raspberries, 118
root-knot nematodes, 76
rosemary, 121
rust, 88

S

sage, 122
seed starting mix, 38
seeding and transplanting, 37

selecting and starting seeds, 37
shallow hoeing, 52
slugs, 76
snails, 76
soil fertility management, 59
soil pH level, 35
spider mites, 76
spinach, 113
springtails, 76
squash bugs, 77
staking plants, 56
starting a no-till garden from scratch, 26
starting a raised bed garden, 31
starting no-till garden beds, 27
starting seeds indoors, 38
storage conditions for vegetables and fruits, 99
storing your harvest, 99
strawberries, 118
succession planting, 19
sun exposure, 17
sun requirements for plants, 17
support for tall or vining plants, 56

T

tender crops, 20
thrips, 77
thyme, 122
tobacco hornworms, 77
tobacco mosaic virus, 91
tomato hornworms, 77
tomato spotted wilt virus, 91
tomatoes, 114
transitioning to no-till, 28
transplanting seedlings, 43
trap cropping for pest control, 82
trap crops, 82
types of fertilizers, 61

V

verticillium wilt, 89
vine weevils, 78
viral diseases, 90

W

watering in-ground gardens, 48
watering raised beds, 50
weeding, 52
whiteflies, 78

Z

zucchini, 115

Printed in Great Britain
by Amazon